Quilting
and
Appliqué
with
Southwest Indian Designs

Charlotte Christiansen Bass

Naturegraph Publishers

Library of Congress Cataloging-in-Publication Data

Bass, Charlotte Christiansen.
Quilting and Appliqué with Southwest Indian Designs / by Charlotte Christiansen Bass.
   p.   cm.
   Includes bibliographical references and index.
   ISBN 0-87961-251-7 (aik. paper)
   1. Quilting—Patterns. 2. Appliqué—Patterns. 3. Indian craft. 4.Indians oF North America—Southwest,
   New.   I. Title.
TT835.B29   1998
746.46′041—dc21   98-7403
                                                            CIP

Artistic credits: All full-body photographs, including front and back covers, are by Edward E. Weiss of Granger, Indiana. Technical line drawings are by Joyce Keane, Studio II, and H. Dean Golding (quilt frame), both of LaPorte, Indiana. In-progress photographs and some line drawings are by the author. Cover design by Av-tek.

Front cover: Indian Motherhood from the collection of Alice and Fred Rippe, Blue Island, Il (34" X 44"). Pattern on page 74.

Back cover: The Eagle! (92" X 82"). The eagle with its grace and power was a coveted symbol among American tribes.

Naturegraph Publishers has been publishing books
on natural history, Native Americans,
and outdoor subjects since 1946.
Please write for our free catalog.

Naturegraph Publishers, Inc.
3543 Indian Creek Road
Happy Camp, CA 96039
(530) 493-5353

Books for a better world

Dedication

This book is dedicated to all Native Americans, to those seeking knowledge about quilting—may their interest soar as the eagle to ever greater heights—and to those who research American Indian artistry and do it justice when using it in their own handcrafts. Finally, this book is dedicated to my husband of fifty-plus years, Colonel Ralph A. Bass, United States Air Force, retired, whose patience allowed me to travel, research countless books, and attend powwows and festivals to serve my need for knowledge. And, I am so glad he can cook!

Charlotte's Quilters Pledge

I, _____, promise to think only happy thoughts when I begin my first Native American quilted tapestry. I will never say "I can't." It's not in my vocabulary. I will only say: "I can!" While quilting, I will smile, not frown. I will not become frustrated seeking perfection. I want success first, as that is more important. *After all, no one was born knowing how to quilt!*

For those of you who have any questions or comments you wish to address to the author, please write to me. My address is: Lilac Manor Farm, 5013 East—450 South, La Porte, Indiana, 46350.

Charlotte Christianen Bass

Acknowledgements

All efforts have been made to obtain permissions from copyright holders to reproduce line drawings and text. I would like to thank the following for allowing me to use their work: (Please see Bibliography for publishers.)

Bertha Dutton and Caroline Olin for Shalako, A Zuni Little Dancer, Zuni Corn Maidens, and Pueblo Prayer Stick in *Myths and Legends of the Indians of the Southwest*. David Rickman for reference to *Plains Indians Coloring Book*, p. 42. A. G. Smith and Josie Hazen for Crow Mother and Eagle Kachina in *Cut and Make Kachina Dolls*. Dorothy Smith-Sides for plates 37a, c, and d, and 48b and c in *Decorative Art of the Southwestern Indians*. Eugene Baatsoslanii Joe and Mark Bahti for interpretations of Father Sky and Mother Earth in *Navajo Sandpainting Art*, p. 21. Donna Greenlee for Kweo, Symbols, and Hano Koshari Glutton in *The Kachina Doll Book*, no. 2, pp. 17, 29, 31. Paul E. Kennedy for Yei Sandpainting in *North American Indian Design Coloring Book*, p. 11. Clair Artimus Millett for Kwahu, Kerwan, Hakto, Momo, Mongwa, Humis, Sip-Ikne, Polik Mana, and Macibol in *Hopi and Zuni Kachina Dancers Coloring Book*. David Villaseñor for Indian Motherhood in *Tapestries in Sand*. David and Jean Villaseñor for Father Sky and Mother Earth and various Indian designs in *Indian Designs*.

Table of Contents

Chapter 1: Colors Live Now and Forever 7
  Native American Color Beliefs 8
    Red 8
    Yellow 9
    Blue 9
    White 10
    Black 10
    Green 10
  The Harmony of Colors 10

Chapter 2: Native American Symbolism 13
    The Eagle 14
    Buffalo 14
    The Rainbow 14
    The Bear 14
    The Wolf 14
    The Owl 15
    The Snake 15
    The Peace Pipe 15
  More Symbolism 15

Chapter 3: Fabric Picture Creation 19
  Locating Designs to Please You 19
  Making a Pattern for Quilting or Appliqué . . 20

Chapter 4: Things That are "Sew" Important 23
  Selecting Fabrics 23
    Cotton 23
    Palencia 23
    Challis 24
    Silk 24
    Velveteen 24
    Tissue Lamé 24
    Taffeta 25
  Washing and Cleaning Fabrics 25
  Pins and Needles 25
  Thread 26
  Hoops 27
  The Thimble 27
  Pencils, Markers, and Erasers 28
  Embroidery Floss 28
  Batting 29

Chapter 5: The Ins and Outs of Applique 31
    Regular Appliqué 32
    Reverse Appliqué 32
    Double Reverse Appliqué 32
  Appliqué: Getting Started 32
  Charlotte's Magic Backstitch 33

Chapter 6: Tips on Background Layout and Design . 35
  The Sashing 35
  A Quick Bias Cutting Method 37
  The Bias Insert 37
  Making Cording 38
  Cutting and Trimming Excess Fabric 39

Chapter 7: The Simple Truth About Quilting 41
  Pencil Quilt Lines 41
  Charlotte's Quick Quilting Technique 43
  The Size of Quilting Stitches 44
  Quilting with a Floor Frame 44
  Quilting with a Hoop 46
  Cutting and Trimming 46
  Counterpane or Wholecloth Quilting 46
  Finding a Quilting Teacher 48

Chapter 8: Adding Hanging Sleeves or Straps . . . 49
  Hanging Sleeves 49
  Hanging Straps 50

Chapter 9: Finish Binding, Mitred Corners, and Final Embellishments 53
  Sewing Down the Binding 53
  About a Mitred Corner 54
  Stuffing the Bias Binding and Finishing . . . 55
  Embellishments Take Imagination 55
    Kachina Neck Ruffs 56

Chapter 10: Patterns to Please You 57
  How to Make a Wolf-Kachina Appliquéd
    Wall Hanging 57
    Wolf Quilt Color Chart 58
    Wolf Quilt Yardage Requirements 60
    Stay-Stitching and Pattern Layout on the
      Straight of Fabric 60
    Making the Wolf's Head, Teeth, and
      Tongue. 61
    Making the Rest of the Wolf Figure 61
    Wolf Background Fabric, Sashing, and
      Quilt Back 62
  How-Hakto, Man-Who-Carries-Wood-on-His-Head
    (Zuni) 63
  Mongwa, The Great Horned Owl (Hopi) . . 64
  Arapaho Lodgemaker 65
  Chief Dancer (Sioux) 66
  Clermont (Osage chief) 67
  Dancing Kwahu—The Eagle Kachina I (Hopi) 68
  The Eagle Kachina II 69
  Crow Mother (Hopi) 70

Hano Kachina, The Clown I (Hopi, Zuni,
   Navajo) 71
Hano Kachina, The Clown II 72
Humis (or Hemis) Kachina (Hopi) 73
Indian Motherhood (Navajo) 74
Father Sky and Mother Earth I (Navajo) . . . 75
Father Sky and Mother Earth II 76
Kerwan, The Bean Planter (Hopi) 77
Macibol, The Serpent Dancer (Hopi) 78
Momo, The Bee Kachina (Zuni) 79
Polik Mana, Butterfly Maiden (Hopi) 80
Pawnee Warrior 81
Sacagawea (Shoshone) 82
Shalako (or Salako), The Rain God (Zuni) . . 83
Sip-Ikne (or Talmopya Akya), The Hummingbird
   (Zuni) 84
Navajo Yei 85
Navajo Rainbow 86
Zuni Corn Maidens 87
A Zuni Little Dancer 88

Appendix: How to Make a Quilt Frame 89
   Materials List 89
   Assembly Instructions 89
Glossary   93

Selected Bibliography 95

Chapter 1:
Colors Live Now and Forever

Colors deep changing hues
Heralding the coming views,
Colors pale, colors bright,
Prisms splitting shafts of light.
Gaze aloft, spirits seen...
Misting showers, earth is green.

— The Rainbow — C. Ann McGuire, Blackfoot

Stand in front of a daylight window. Close your eyes! Squeeze them together. You see black! While still closed, relax them. You might see gray or red. Now open them wide and a world of color is before you. Statement: without light there is no color. Colors are exciting. Use them freely in your quilts. Purchasing color fabrics costs no more than purchasing boring non-colors!

Going back to the time of Sir Isaac Newton (1746–1727) and his experiments with glass prisms, he discovered that a small shaft of light passing through one would always relay the colors in the same order: red, orange, yellow, blue, green, and violet. Same as a rainbow!

Color is light, a wavelength coming from or reflected by an object. There are three primary colors: red, yellow, and blue. All contain white, but red and blue contain black. If a fabric contains a bit of black in its color composition, its hue will change according to the time of day and the light coming onto it. For example, lilac can appear as lilac on a sunny day or a dusty pink or gray on a cloudy day.

Use all the color possible in your quilts. Use bright, happy, and uplifting colors that make you feel good, like the rainbow colors. Basic beige is no fun! The rainbow's exciting colors always appear in the same pattern as in Newton's experiment. When there is a double rainbow, the color order is reversed.

Native American Color Beliefs

Colors are not incidental in Native American rituals and handcrafts. They have meanings which reflect the long-established beliefs and traditions of particular tribes. The colors used by all tribes usually fall into four categories: 1) war and peace symbolism, 2) ceremonies, 3) death and mourning, and 4) decorative purposes. Many Indians believed colors had power, and by using them they would be protected or grow spiritually. Southwest peoples made their own dyes from natural products, and stored the colors in special pieces of pottery. The color depth of their dyes depended on what mordant (dye setter) was used. Often the most available mordant was human urine.

The range of dyes and pigments in use among Indian tribes was not great. It was their ingenuity that produced lovely earth-tone colors with the help of roots, leaves, blossoms, bark, cones, bugs, sand, clay, and rock. It wasn't until white traders with their gaudy European goods arrived on the scene that bright hues became prevalent. Indians found many dyes and other items easier to obtain by trading than making them from scratch.

RED: This was the most frequently used color. It is still prevalent in powwows, ceremonial events, dances, and as a body decoration. It represented courage, life, fire, blood, sunsets, and protection. To the Sioux and other Plains tribes it was a sacred color, the color of the earth from which everything increases. The Aztecs made red dye from a female wood louse known as cochineal, which planted itself on cacti and stayed their because the female was wingless. The insects were swept into hot water, dried in the sun, and then powdered. Various colors can be made from this wood louse depending on the dye setter used. Today, cochineal dye is highly priced and it has become an artist's staple along with red madder. Other sources of red were pokeberry, safflower, pussywillow buds, red clay, and St. John's wort. Red dye was mixed with buffalo, bear, or deer grease to make paint, or the body was coated with one of these grease products and the powders were applied. Warriors of the Plains tribes would apply red paint to their faces

Chief Dancer - Sioux *moves slowly and stately to show his authority as tribal leader.*
From the collection of Mary Porter Browne, Niles, Michigan

KWAHU, The Eagle Kachina - Hopi *imitates the movements and rhythm of the eagle in flight.*

HANO the Glutton Clown - Zuni, Hopi & Navajo *makes fun with mysterious movements for the audience to laugh after serious ceremonies.*

HANO the Thin Clown - Zuni, Hopi, & Navajo, *like the Glutton Clown, also makes fun to relax and amuse the audience after witnessing serious, sacred ceremonies.*

SHALAKO, A Zuni Rain God Messenger *dances at special ceremonies to bring rain, thus making the land fruitful for corn, squash, and beans.*

and bodies before a battle. Indian maidens often applied red in their hair part and on their faces to attract a man.

YELLOW: After red, yellow was the most widely used color because of its availability. It was made by combining buffalo gallstones, moss from pine trees, or powdered earth with the roots of certain plants to create the desired shade. Goldenseal root, dock, Osage orange, sumac roots, and hemlock bark all produced yellow. Also, sunflower or coneflower petals boiled with cattail or oak bark produced yellow. Yellow represented love, prosperity, gaiety, and fidelity. It was also used for the sun, gold, corn, daylight, earth, energy, and strength. Corn was most sacred to the Hopi and Zuni to whom it represented a mother who produces many children, i.e. the kernels on the cob.

BLUE: This color was obtained from traders or in town stores when reservations were established. On the plains, duck manure was sometimes used for blue. Blue represented solitude, faithfulness, and endurance. It was a symbol for the moon, the sky, wind and clouds, thunder, and water. The Navajo feel the color turquoise is stolen from the sky, and they use this hue a great deal as a symbol of supreme life-giving power. They exchange turquoise for currency and carry it for good luck. A string of turquoise beads at one time could be traded for several horses by the Zuni of western New Mexico. Hopi

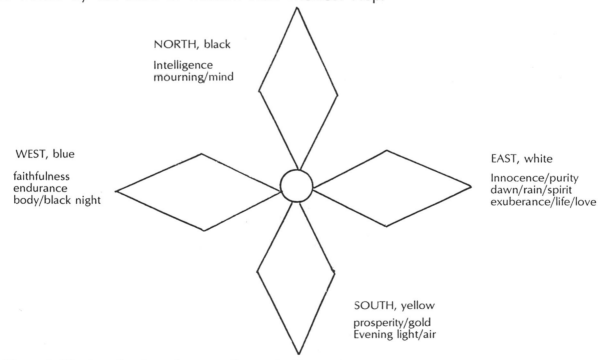

NORTH, black

Intelligence
mourning/mind

WEST, blue

faithfulness
endurance
body/black night

EAST, white

Innocence/purity
dawn/rain/spirit
exuberance/life/love

SOUTH, yellow

prosperity/gold
Evening light/air

Figure 1. The four direction colors according to the Navajo. Direction colors varied widely from tribe to tribe.

and Zuni tribes use blue with white clouds on their kachina head tablets to represent rain, which they need to raise their corn.

WHITE: In their western explorations, Lewis and Clark saw white clay and white earth used for this color. It represented spirit, purity, innocence, exuberance, life, and love. It was a symbol for winter, rain, and dawn. White was used by the Pawnee in the wolf symbol as a help in scouting. The Hopi and Zuni loved white feathers, such as the down of an eagle. White was often used to paint special animals, such as birds, buffalo, deer, and rabbits, on pottery and tipis.

BLACK: Tribes such as the Arapaho, Arikara, Blackfeet, Cheyenne, and Dakotas often used black to illustrate buffalo skin robes and tipis with the stories of battles, heroic deeds, death, victory, and so on. Black represented mourning, protection, and victory. Face and body painting with this color was popular. Face painting before battle did not necessarily have a meaning other than to look mean and frightening to the enemy. Black walnuts, oak galls, black earth, charcoal, and often grapes were used to make this hue.

GREEN: Although representing new life and growth in the spring, this color was not widely used. According to the Ojibwa, green is connected to the south and good crops brought on by warm weather. Leaves of the lily-of-the-valley, copper ore, colored muds, and various water plants were some of the sources for this color.

The study of color is worth your time to understand what Native Americans went through to obtain their dyes. Today, many modern quilters dye their own fabrics and have access to a wide variety of commercial and natural dyes. If you are a purist and wish only to use homemade dye, be sure it is well set with a mordant, such as alum, salt, or vinegar; otherwise, your dye will run or fade and all your effort will be wasted.

The Harmony of Colors

Native Americans made art pieces to stand out against firelight or the open sky. This is similar to matting a picture with a complimentary color to make a well-rounded composition. Don't put a brown piece on top of a beige background if you want imaginative contrast. Use a light green or white background.

To quilters harmony means structure, and colors contrasting pleasantly together, not fighting each other. Colors should inspire excitement, but in a complimentary

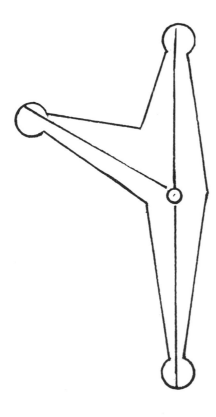

Figure 2. Color-wheel dial.

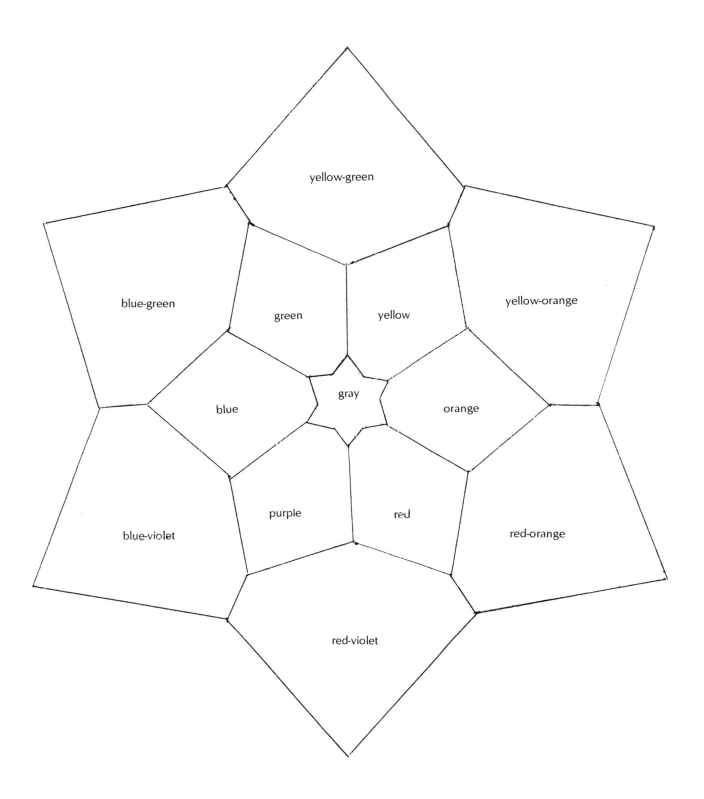

Figure 2a. The color-wheel star.

way, as in a perfectly performed concert or chorus. In modern art, to the contrary, some lines may be purposely offensive to the eye, and colors often clash, primarily to get your attention by their very repugnance.

The three basic colors of blue, red, and yellow in various hues will "live" with each other. They are complimentary. Blue is complimentary to orange, green to red, and yellow to purple. In the color-wheel star in Figure 2a, each family of colors has another family to its right and left and is opposite its complimentary color family.

Make a copy of the color-wheel star and the color-wheel dial, then cut them out, and use them to help you find complimentary color combinations which are unbelievable. For color-combination ideas, you can also visit a paint store and look at paint color-chips, or, better yet, watch a sunrise or sunset and go from there. Look at the inside of a flower or any other of nature's countless possibilities. Native Americans had great color sense just from living in close contact with nature. They followed what they saw in the coloring of birds, animals, and the land, making their creations pleasant to the eye, soothing to the soul, and very exciting.

One of the most moving events in my life occurred in April 1996 when I was visiting the Zuni reservation in Zuni, New Mexico. Alex Seowtewa and his sons, Kenneth and Edwin, were faithfully restoring the Our Lady of Guadalupe Church at Zuni. When Alex told us of his experiences painting some thirty kachinas on the walls high above the congregation, as well as about the structural restoration, I was moved to tears. Seowtewa's huge kachinas revealed a harmony of colors and authenticity that were totally pleasing to the eye and soothing to my soul. This is what art is all about. In my own work, I also take great care to preserve true Indian colors and to make all of my quilted wall tapestries as authentic as possible. Alex's Shalako inspired my own rendition.

Seek out colors which please you. Don't be inhibited because a fabric isn't 100 percent cotton or blended of 65 percent polyester and 35 percent combed cotton. If the right color is there, that's all that counts. Be thankful you don't have to powder some bugs to attain what you want! I strongly recommend that you include a color wheel, such as the one in Figure 2, in your collection of quilting tools. You'll be glad to have it when you go shopping, and you won't have to depend on a clerk who has no taste for the daring and exciting.

Chapter 2:
Native American Symbolism

And as imagination bodies forth
The forms of things unknown, the poet's pen
Turns them to shapes, and gives to airy nothing
A local habitation and a name.

— Midsummer Night's Dream — William Shakespeare,

The treasury of Native American symbolism is filled with wondrous shapes that have deep and beautiful meanings. Long before Columbus discovered America, symbolism in art thrived across the known world among peoples of all national origins. Symbolism was especially important to tribes with no written language. A story of the past was drawn on tipi walls, inside and out; weapons and pottery were etched with symbols; walls in canyons were carved or painted with pictographs. The Hmong from Laos In southeast Asia had no written language, but they recorded their history in magnificent needlework long before the Vietnam conflict. Today, the Smithsonian Institution in Washington, DC, as well as the Library of Congress, collect quilts, tapestries, and embroidery as documentation of history. Much of this work has been translated for posterity.

When an Indian created something, there was always a threefold purpose: 1) to be manageable and lasting, 2) to have a true function, and 3) to stimulate spiritual feelings. Symbolism was the key to the last purpose. A wavy line for water represented life and movement. A pyramid shape for mountains represented strength. Circles for the sun and the moon symbolized harmony. All of nature—mineral, vegetable, and animal—symbolized something greater than itself. Natural images represented meanings and emotions of profound significance.

Red dot = killed an enemy
(often many dots)

Cut an enemy's throat

Taken scalps

Each cut = an enemy kill

Figure 3. The meaning of feather markings.

THE EAGLE: Many tribes considered the eagle to be the spirit of their dead, and believed that wind was created by the flapping of its wings. Its power of flight brought it into close relation with the Great Spirit. Because eagles only produce two eggs, many believed this to be a sign that all things come in two: good and evil, fair and ugly, daylight and darkness, right and left. The black and white, or brown and white, colors of the coveted eagle were associated with the pair of night and day. The eagle is still a symbol of power and pride, and wearing an eagle feather represents the bird's strength and speed. Clipped feathers in various designs mean specific things. The hawk was also considered to be a bird of strength, and it was believed that courage in battle came from these birds.

BUFFALO: The Plains Indians never wasted any portion of a buffalo, which they considered a sacred being. The meat was eaten fresh as well as dried for winter food. Clothing, blankets, and tipi covers came from buffalo skins. Sinew provided thread and string, and from the bones and horns tools were made. Even the tails decorated the exterior of the tipi. In other words, everything necessary for survival was contained within the buffalo. It is no wonder that when white men would kill the buffalo and let their carcasses remain unused on the prairie, the Indians would become enraged.

THE RAINBOW: In the Navajo sandpainting in Figure 4, there is a very elongated figure with its head at one end and the torso bottom at the other end. The space between is the rainbow. This unusual configuration encircles and "guards" the work contained inside. Its opening must always face east, where evil cannot enter, and protect north, south, and west. Rainbows foretell that the weather is changing. As a symbol, it was often painted on the face of warriors as a bridge to another world and to help carry them over a great body of water. The medicine men of many tribes included rainbows in their prayers to obtain healing from them.

THE BEAR: Bears were honored. They were considered very wise and strong. The bear-paw mark was also painted on the face of warriors, and tales of encounters with bears were described on tipis. Even in today's old-fashioned quilting circles, the bear-paw pattern is popular. See Figure 5.

THE WOLF: Wearing a wolf skin and head was not uncommon on hunts among the Zuni, Hopi, and Navajo. It represented courage and resourcefulness. Wolves can quietly endure the worst of conditions. The wolf kachina, or deity, was believed to communicate with warriors via their actions. The wolf was well regarded both in serious ceremonies and clownish activities. Wolf-paw marks are seen throughout the Indian art world.

THE OWL: Medicine men considered the owl a symbol of wisdom. Headpieces as well as wings of owls are worn and carried in ceremonies to this day. The Kiowa believed that if they heard an owl hoot, it was a sign they would return home safely.

THE SNAKE: The snake represented a spear of war and a god of lightning. Its movements were thought to have magical powers. It was also known as the god of fruitfulness and the bringer of rain. It was well-known as a war charm and was often painted on warriors' bodies or clothing. Snakes were often beaded on moccasins to protect the wearer against snake bite.

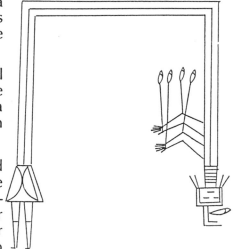

Figure 4. The Yei, or rainbow, surrounds some sandpaintings.

THE PEACE PIPE: Smoking the peace pipe was a very serious ceremony with rules for who smokes first and which direction the pipe goes around the tipi. The use of tobacco, the creation of the pipe, and its markings all have special meanings. See Figure 6.

More Symbolism

Medicine bundles were worn about the neck or in a side-belt hip bag, and contained many articles, such as soft eagle feathers to represent the sun, the skin of a weasel for quick movement, a disk bone from an animal to represent the sun, and so forth. Often times wing pieces of various birds were carried and used in dances and ceremonies. Some believed that birds were spirits of the deceased, or messengers from sky deities which could produce wind, water spouts, and clouds because of their swiftness. The hummingbird, the mourning dove, the crow, the eagle, and the hawk were all honored.

Scalps hung on tipis, coup sticks, and belts were marks of bravery. Today, instead of real scalps, braids of woven green grass worn at the belt are used to represent scalps.

The sun as the source of life-giving light and warmth was a common symbol for the Great Spirit. The Arapaho called him "Man Above"; the Crow "First Maker"; and the Blackfoot "Man-Who-Travels-From-East-to-West." The sun in the sky was also the wife of the Moon Father, and the Morning Star (Venus), the son of the sun and the moon. The Pawnee believed the Evening Star (Venus) protected crops during planting time. These three sym-

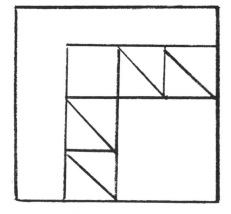

Figure 5. The bear-paw mark and a traditional bear-paw quilt pattern.

bols make gorgeous appliqué designs for a quilted wall tapestry or border of a quilt.

Native Americans recorded their history with symbols. The squash blossom represented fertility; hearing the mourning dove, with its plaintive coo, was a sacred sound. The swan symbolized the four cardinal directions: north, south, east, and west. A spiderweb was often found painted or embroidered on children's clothing as protection against the supernatural.[1] Black circle tattoos were done in the middle of an Indian woman's forehead representing the sun and daytime, and a four-pointed star was placed on her cheek for the nighttime sky.

When studying Indian lore, of primary importance is to get it right. Respect their ways and make an honest attempt to interpret their work correctly. Keep colors true and symbolism correct.

The Indian design you cut out and sew onto the central piece of fabric is your appliqué decoration. This should be complemented with symbolic designs matching the colors of your creation. Figures 7 and 7a show some examples of symbols you might want to use. You can increase their size and use them as quilting patterns on the border, or at each corner of your work. Lastly, add straight or curved fill lines to help complete the meaning of your quilted wall tapestry. These "hidden" fill lines bring a work to life. It is fun to stand beside your accomplishment and ask an admiring viewer: "What else do you see beyond the figure?" You might want to remember this for yourself. It's amazing what we miss by not looking beyond what we think we see.

Figure 6. The peace pipe, often decorated rather than plain.

---

1 During the Industrial Revolution in the 1850s, spider webs were often included on "crazy quilts" as part of a rage of "new" types of handiwork.

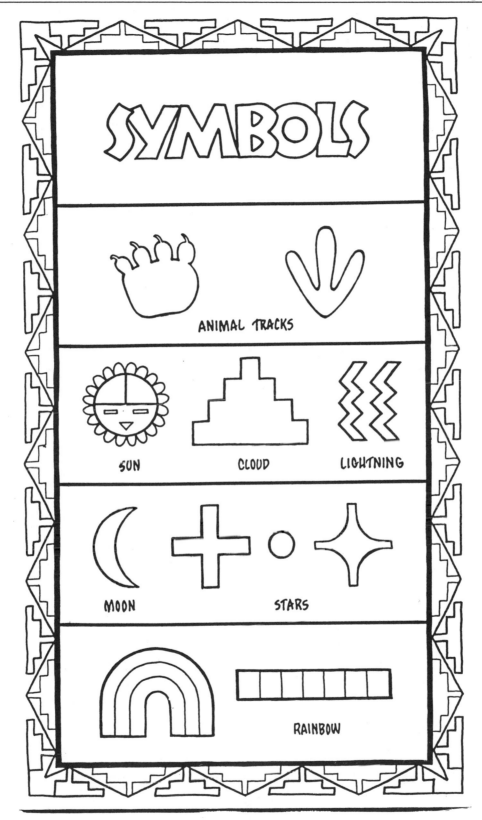

Figure 7. Indian symbols.

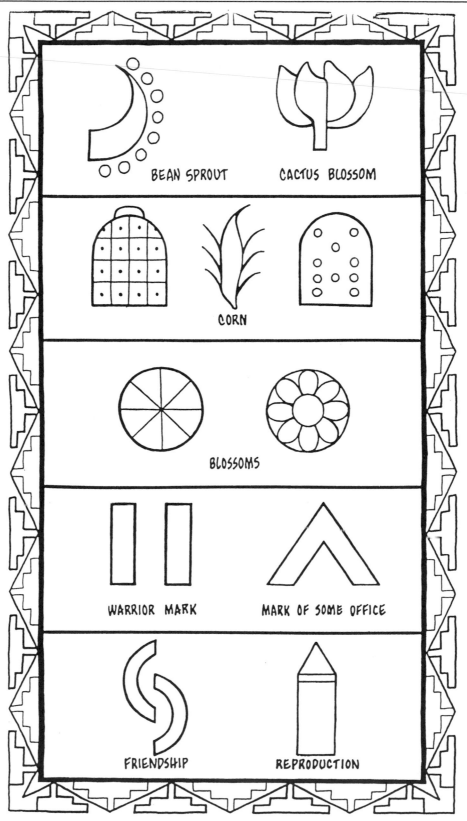

Figure 7a. Indian symbols

Chapter 3
Fabric Picture Creation

And dreams of that which cannot die,
Bright visions came to me,
As lapped in thought I used to lie
And gaze into the summer sky...

Henry Wadsworth Longfellow

A "bright vision" came to me about doing Indian quilting, though I had no idea how to do it, after a friend of mine, Joyce Keane, told me about an Indian art show she and a pottery artist were scheduled to present. I suggested a tipi would be a neat focal point. You know what happens when you volunteer suggestions! One week later I had completed a three dimensional, quilted tipi. The tipi is made in a six-foot half circle and has twelve foot long poles. Trying to find out how to make a tipi took the most time, but a Boy Scout handbook did the trick. To make sure everything was in the right proportion, I made a model tipi out of paper at a ratio of one inch to one foot. On the tipi, for which I used earthtone colors, I appliquéd stars, moon, butterflies, buffalo, mountains, and rain. The flaps were added after the tipi was quilted. Since then I have made another tipi. This one is also six feet tall, but it hangs flat to the wall with a curved curtain rod at the bottom so it has a three-dimensional appearance. Now, some thirty-five Indian quilts later, the tips and short-cuts I developed are presented in this book.

Locating Designs to Please You

Getting started making a quilt or a quilted wall hanging is very easy. First, you need to do research to find a picture or pattern you like. I do research for every one-woman art show I present at various galleries. Some of my collections include: Ancient Egypt in Stitches, China in Silk, the 200th Anniversary of the Circus in America, Angels in Outer Space, Modern Norway, and Christopher Columbus and His Ships. The most fun I had was when I was national spokesperson for the 100th anniversary of the Statue of Liberty Great America Quilt Show held in New York in 1985! The pieces in all my collections required preliminary research to make them authentic representations of the themes involved.

Borrowing patterns or designs is nothing new. Quilters see a pattern and then use it to create their own pattern, often rendering it in a way different from the original. Throughout this book you will find interesting designs Indians used that can easily be adapted to your own stitching ideas. Inspiring design ideas can be found in numerous sources: books, magazines, post cards, trips, events, collections, museum art, and so forth. The possibilities are unlimited.

In general, my designs in this book have come from coloring books on Indians and other wonderful "real" sources. I am especially fascinated by the kachina figures of the Hopi, Zuni, and Navajo. Each trip I have taken to the Southwest has only whetted my appetite to learn more about them.

Making a Pattern for Quilting or Appliqué

How do you make a pattern for quilting or appliqué? One way is to handcopy designs, making them larger. The easiest way is to use a photocopy machine at a local business to enlarge the picture to about one-third of the final design size. Then use a medium-width, black magic marker to outline the subject's prominent lines. Do not include too much detail. Let some of the shadow lines fall out; otherwise the pattern will be too complicated to manage (see Figure 8).

You may need to add some muscle lines. Next, trace the dark lines you have drawn on the machine-made copy on a piece of tracing paper. This is your first master pattern.

Go back to the copy machine and enlarge the pattern to suit your needs. (This may require that you tape the pieces together.) Always have more positive design than negative in your work. In other words, make the central image large enough so it will not be dwarfed by the background, and make the background area small enough so that the central figure is suitably emphasized.

For appliqué work, a figure should be about thirty-six inches tall. When you enlarge your final pattern, make two copies: one to cut apart patterns, i.e. legs, body, head, etc., to layout on your various colored fabrics, and the other as a master on which to place your fabrics when you are ready to do appliqué. Identify each pattern piece that you cut and indicate the piece of fabric it goes with. (See Figure 37.)

For wholecloth quilting, if you wish to embroider a design on a solid piece of fabric, prepare your master pattern as suggested, and simply place the paper pattern beneath the background fabric (a light color so you can see the pattern beneath it), and trace on the pattern. Then use two strands of floss in a single color, or merely quilt in the design without embroidery at all.

NOTE: If you elect not to make an appliqué quilt for starters, but would prefer to embroider the Indian design directly on a wholecloth quilt, read Chapter 4, and then go directly to Chapter 7 on quilting.

A

B

Figure 8. Tracing a buffalo pattern.

Chapter 4:
Things That are "Sew" Important

Sermons and epigrams have a like end
To improve, to reprove, and to amend.
Some pass without this use 'cause they are witty;
And so do many sermons, more's the pity!

— *The Reader* — *1628 Robert Hayman*

Selecting Fabrics

COTTON: Many quilters do not realize that a new era has opened in the past decade in the quality of fabrics for quilt projects. Not long ago if a material was called calico and marked 100 percent cotton, the material wasn't very good. The weave was too far apart, colors weren't "fast," fading was a huge problem, raveling after washing was dismaying, and ironing would cause the fabric to lose its shape. This is why I used only blended fabrics and still do most of the time. My time is too valuable!

I have amended my thinking somewhat now. Today, there are very fine cottons on the market that approach the quality of fifty years ago. I even use a few cotton prints, but never a solid cotton color. This is a very open-minded statement for me, as I am basically anti-cotton for quilts. Most of the new, quality cottons cost between $8 and $10 a yard. That's expensive.

PALENCIA: My favorite fabric is Palencia, a combed broadcloth made by Springs Industries. It doesn't fade, wrinkle, beard (referring to batting coming through the quilt because the fabric is too loosely woven), or fray at the edges. Palencia is a blend of 65 percent polyester and 35 percent combed cotton. It sells from about $1.87 to $4.69 a yard. My first quilt made out of Palencia has yet to fade.

CHALLIS: This is a soft rayon type of fabric. Underlay it with a piece of batiste for more body and to avoid bearding.

SILK: This is a wonderful and luxurious fabric excellent for framing under glass. The sheen is glorious! If the silk is very thin, you should underlay it with silk organza. Silk is fragile and takes up body oil quickly with handling, so have clean hands. To preserve the silk longer, add a breathing hole at the back of the frame and don't allow the glass to touch the silk. When pressing, use a very cool iron because it scorches quickly.

VELVETEEN: Use cotton velveteen, not chiffon velvet, as the latter is difficult to handle. If using a small portion of velveteen on the top side of the quilt, mark the quilting lines with a yellow artist's pencil and handle as little as possible, as the nap eats up the lines. If doing a wholecloth velveteen quilt with a design, mark the *back* of the fabric sandwich and quilt on the backside. In other words, your quilt sandwich will include: (1) the velveteen, (2) the batting, and (3) the backing. It is the backing that is marked. The stitches on the front will disappear, more or less, in the velveteen nap. The end result will be glorious! CAUTION: Do not let a velveteen quilt remain in the hoop too long as the nap (pile) will become crushed.

Cotton velveteen should be handled with the nap running upwards. In other words, if you are standing with it in front of you (hanging down on your body), it should be rough when you rub your hand downward. The color is more defined in this position. Turned the other way, with the nap running down, the color is cloudy. This applies to corduroy as well.

TISSUE LAMÉ: As the weave on tissue lamé is loose and the fabric so thin, always put another color underlay beneath it and handle them both as one piece of fabric; otherwise, the batting will beard.

When using an underlay with lamé, I use a bright color to give drama to the finished product. On gold I use orange; on silver I use bright blue. Mark your circle (as in the wolf kachina's moon, see color plates), or whatever the design is, on the underlay, and pin that to the lamé. Stitch on the underlay side directly on your pencil lines. To get a circle, a pizza board or a cake pan work well. When marking directly on the topside of lamé, for additional quilting lines, I use a black ballpoint pen. All signs of this mark will disappear in the quilting when it is completed. Using a ballpoint pen applies only to lamé!

Some tips on using lamé. Be certain you have a sharp machine needle in place or the threads will pull or tear. After stay-stitching, cut away any excess fabric, leaving a one-quarter inch seam allowance. Should any pucker or tightness show after this stitching, simply clip a couple of bobbin stitches on the backside and finger press.

Pressing is touchy with lamé because it can melt. If you must press on the top side, use a cool iron (no steam!) and a man's soft handkerchief. I usually press lamé on the underlay side, as there is seldom a reason to press on the top. Be careful when giving the entire appliquéd piece a final press. I only do this just before I am ready to put the side strips, or sashing, in place.

TAFFETA: Taffeta has a wonderful sheen and provides drama. As a springy fabric, it might require an underlay.

Washing and Cleaning Fabrics

I don't wash any of the fabrics I use. Though, after a couple years, I do clean wall hangings without using water if they become dirty. If you do plan to wash your fabrics prior to doing a project, test the material beforehand for color fastness. The easiest way to do this is to clip off some of the fabric, put it in a little water with a piece of white fabric and a piece of soap, and boil it. If it runs, don't use it. All 100 percent cotton, even the expensive varieties, should be checked for color fastness, because cotton tends to run.

Here are the steps I use to clean my quilted tapestries.

1. Carefully shake out the quilt to remove dust, or use a soft brush and go over it.

2. Lay it flat and shake *white* cornmeal all over it. Use a couple cups of cornmeal, more or less, depending on the size of the quilt.

3. Let it stand all night.

4. Shake and brush off the quilt in the morning.

5. The final result: Clean!

Caution: Do not use this technique if the humidity is high.

Pins and Needles

Thin pins are a must. Do not use those monsters with the ball heads. The holes they make are unsightly. I strongly recommend no. 17 silk pins, which can be purchased by the quarter-pound box.

I do not own a quilting needle because my hands are too large and it takes me too much time dealing with something so small. Instead, I use a no. 8 or no. 9 crewel embroidery needle for both appliqué and quilting. The eye is longer and easier to thread than a quilting needle, and its shank is longer, so more stitches can be put on with it. Do not use the same needle indefinitely, as a sharp barb develops from wear. The best policy is to change your needles often.

On an average quilt being done on a floor frame, I have about twenty-five to thirty needles going at the same time. As I quilt, I can then move from spot to spot and pick up a needle instead of having to rethread all the time. With my thumb I quilt away from myself, although I use my middle finger sometimes. I do not hold my needle when I quilt. I lean it into my thimble and wiggle it all the way through the quilt layers. By not holding the needle, I do not have those three fingers in the way. It's almost like an automatic transmission in a car. Push, pull, and go! (See Figure 22.)

Thread

Use poly-wrapped quilting thread for normal durable quilts which will undergo a lot of wear and tear. The stitches will not break when a little tension is placed on them. If doing a baby or youth quilt, a heavy thread is a must. One hundred percent cotton thread with no wrap is too weak. For wall hangings (i.e. my "quilted tapestries"), I use regular dual-duty thread by J. P. Coats. Since quilts hanging on a wall undergo little wear and tear, it is not necessary to use quilting thread for them.

The limited color range of quilt thread makes choices difficult. If making a regular quilt, pick one color of thread and use it throughout a piece instead of mixing up colors depending upon your appliqué colors. It looks better on the backside. But this is where quilting and appliqué part company. Perfect thread color match is imperative for appliqué tapestries. Don't worry about the different thread colors showing on the backside, as no one is going to see your stitches, unless they try to peak when you're not looking. You can always install a mousetrap in back of your wall hanging for nosey fingers!

Metallic threads in quilted wall hangings are wonderful. They are not suitable for quilts in daily use; they are strictly for drama on wall pieces. DMC or Talon are two brands that take the pull I put on my stitches. Most other brands break too easily. Use short thread lengths of about eight or nine inches. The ply will become unraveled if threads are too long. Do not use a rolled spit knot. Hand-tie a single knot at the end where you cut it off of the spool. All metallic threads should be handled in this manner. For quilting and regular threads, put the knot opposite the end where it is cut off (see Figure 9).

Hoops

All of my embroidery and appliqué is done on two different-sized, plastic oval hoops. I use either a small 4½ x 6 inch oval or a 5 x 9 inch oval. Both have screw tensions. A round hoop is perfectly all right as well, but I find the oval hoop faster to maneuver and not so difficult to handle. While doing embroidery and appliqué, I handle my hoop right-side up. For quilting, however, I handle the hoop upside down, i.e., with the screw-tension hoop on the bottom.

For quilting, I use a 10 x 20 inch oval hoop with screw tension. I place my quilt sandwich on top of it and press the plain hoop down to secure the sandwich. I give the quilt a little push in the middle to ease the tension, then tighten up the screws underneath. Having less tension on the fabric gives me speed in quilting. The same applies when using the floor frame. Too tight a tension makes for very slow quilting. The reason I handle this hoop upside down is because the fabric becomes additionally taut if you hold the hoop right-side up. But upside down, you grasp the wood, not the top of the quilt itself (see Figure 10). Also, by holding it upside down, there is a place to keep the thread and thimble.

The Thimble

There isn't anyone who used to hate thimbles more than myself, unless it was you. A wonderful Amish lady, Hazel Bellinger, who taught me to quilt, noticed one day that I did not use a thimble. She said to me: "Take it along; you'll find something to do with it." In the beginning, I tried a leather finger from a glove with a soft-drink tab inserted in it. It was okay. While teaching at Purdue University, one of my students (Dean Golding) saw my dilemma. In the second class he attended, he came with something similar to what is on the market today. Between the two of us, Finger's Friend, the velcro-closing leather thimble was born. It has a piece of metal in the center for strength. The secret to using this thimble successfully is its fitting.

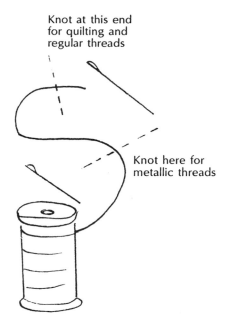

Knot at this end for quilting and regular threads

Knot here for metallic threads

Figure 9. Where to knot your threads.

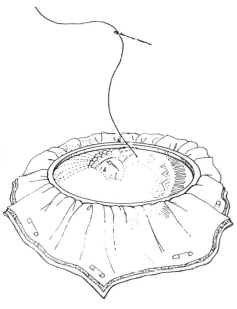

Figure 10. Quilting with the hoop upside down. The right side of the work shows in this illustration.

I close the flaps on the back of my thumb at an angle (similar to the way a Chinese squeeze finger works). This way I can move it easily from my thumb to the middle finger as necessary, depending upon which direction my quilting lines take me. I readjust the velcro only when the leather stretches.

I use the thimble on my thumb when doing appliqué, as the leather allows me to pull the needle through quickly and safely. No bloody fingers at my house. (Note: If you do get a spot of blood on your work, take a small piece of white thread, moisten it with your saliva, and then rub it across the spot. It will disappear like magic. Or use club soda for the same result.) While I use this thimble exclusively, I do not have it on to begin or end my work, when I need my fingers free and clear.

Another tip: When doing heavy quilting hour after hour, for protection I put clear tape on my index finger over a small piece of the plastic lid of the needle case. It works. I also put tape on my middle finger, which feels the needle underneath the quilting frame. I never have sore fingers!

Pencils, Markers, and Erasers

Don't use quilt markers that claim their marks disappear. They will come back on a moist day. Instead, mark your quilting lines with a no. 1 or no. 2, regular lead pencil. (Automatic lead pencils are too sharp and don't work well.) Do not mark lines too heavily, and do not mark them with short strokes. Hold your pencil half way up. You will have better control and the lines will be neater (see Figure 11). Don't worry about the pencil being on the fabric. The lines will disappear in the shadows, especially if you use Fatt Batt.

Never use the eraser on top of a lead pencil to erase pencil lines on your fabric. Doing this usually leaves a dirty red mark. Purchase a plastic artist's eraser, which will remove lines effectively. If not available, take a piece of the same fabric you are erasing and use it like an eraser. It will usually take out the pencil lines.

Embroidery Floss

My preference in embroidery floss is DMC 6-strand cotton. I use two of the six strands when embroidering to add emphasis and drama to the quilt. I usually quilt next to those embroidered lines for excitement. Any color can be used to coordinate with your fabrics. I prefer black. I

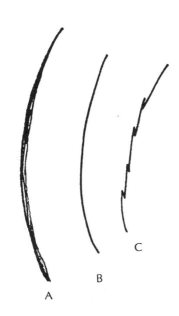

Figure 11. Pencil lines: (A) too heavy and dark; (B) just right; (C) poor.

use a single strand of floss for signing, dating, and giving a title to my work. Don't just include your initials, and when writing the year, put in all the numbers! Practice on a piece of paper first for spacing. Open all the letters in your handwriting, as it is easier to embroider.

Batting

There are many quilt batting brands on the market. Some come on huge rollers to be purchased by the yard. I avoid these as they are usually not wide enough to accommodate the sizes of my projects. Besides cotton batting, which doesn't provide many shadows, polyester, wool, silk, and black batting are also available. My exclusive choice for a batting is Mountain Mist Fatt Batt, which has lovely loft and makes great shadows. It performs for me, and I can depend on it. Often when I need some batting with less thick loft, such as when working with silk, I tear the Fatt Batt gently down the middle to obtain a piece half as thick. Occasionally, I also stretch it to obtain a slightly thinner piece.

Remove batting from the package and unroll it about a week before you use it. This lets it expand so the wrinkles are not as bad and will not distort the quilt top and bottom fabrics. This batt is usually used for tied comforters or coverlets, and I don't know of anyone else who uses it the way I do, except for my students. Hint: When using Fatt Batt, stretch it gently when laying it on the back of the quilt. As with any batting, it may be heavier in some areas.

When joining batting pieces, don't sew them together, as this is unnecessary. Butting one side to the other is also useless, because during the quilting process they usually separate and you'll have a space with nothing. Instead, tear the edges of the two pieces to be joined and lap one over the other. They will stick together.

What are a pair of blue jeans doing in a book about Indian quilts? They show familiar examples of appliqué and reverse appliqué.

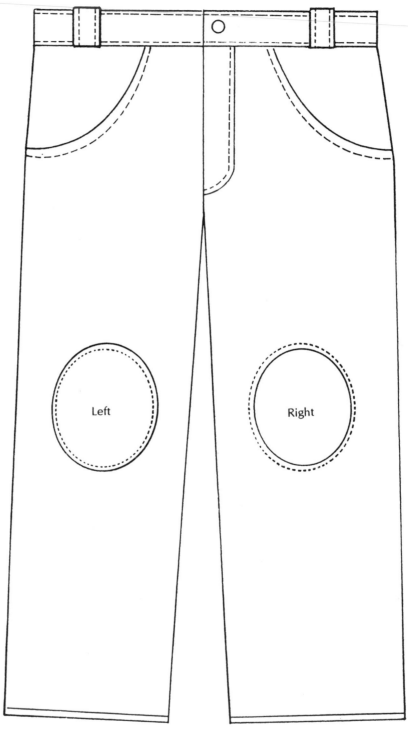

Figure 12. The jeans show a quick example of appliqué and reverse appliqué. **Left:** *Regular appliqué. An oval patch has been put on top of the hole and the stitch is on the oval.* **Right:** *Reverse appliqué. An oval has been placed under the hole (on the inside) and the stitch is on the jeans itself.*

Chapter 5:
The Ins and Outs of Appliqué

Why thus longing, thus forever sighing,
For the far-off, unattained and dim,
While the beautiful, all round thee lying,
Offers up its low, perpetual hymn.

Harriet Winslow, nineteenth century

If you want to do fine appliqué, the fulfillment of your wish is at hand. There are many ins and outs to this ancient method of fabric decoration. The most important step at this point is to decide what background piece to use on which you will sew your appliqué figure. The background piece should complement the size, color, and shape of your central figure appliqué. Do not let the background dwarf the subject. A general rule of thumb is to leave about six inches of space on either side and at the bottom of the central figure and about eight inches at the top. This does not include any side sashing you might add. See the sizes on my quilts pictured in this book for an idea.

Cut the background fabric and ensure the squareness of its corners. You can do this with a posterboard by placing it along the selvage (hard woven side of fabric). If the edge is not a pure square, mark it with a pencil and trim to make it even. Make certain your measurements are exact on both sides, top and bottom. Your background fabric is now ready.

Remember, all appliqué work should be done in a hoop for the best control. You need to control the fabric; don't let it control you. As a general rule, the most out-

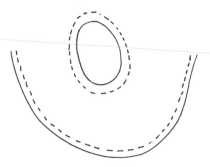

A. Stay-stitching is complete.

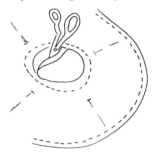

B. Pin another colored fabric under the stay-stitched circle, then trim out the center so it shows through.

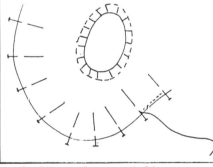

C. Clip to the stay-stitching, not through it. Put more pins in to hold appliqué in place on the quilt top.

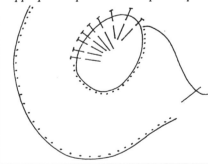

D. Stitch down and use the backstitch for extra strength. Pin ahead of yourself only a couple inches at a time.

Figure 13. Reverse appliqué.

standing prizes and prices at quilting shows and sales are for appliqué work. All of my quilted wall hangings have been done using either regular, reverse, or double reverse appliqué. With the exception of the huge Eagle work, most of them took only about seven days to appliqué, quilt, and bind after the pattern was struck.

REGULAR APPLIQUÉ involves placing a piece of stay-stitched fabric *on top* of the background material, turning under its quarter-inch seam allowance, and then stitching it down (see Figure 12).

REVERSE APPLIQUÉ consists of pinning a piece of fabric *under* a stay-stitched area. Then cut out the material within the stay-stitching, leaving a one-quarter inch seam to be turned under. Stitch down to the circle and then to the quilt top (see figures 12 and 13).

DOUBLE REVERSE APPLIQUÉ is used in the San Blas Indian molas from Panama, where several colors of fabric are all placed under the top layer. What color appears depends on which colors are used and in which order they are cut away. (Beautiful blouses, pillows, and framed handwork in multiple layered reverse appliqué are examples of molas.)

Appliqué: Getting Started

Your master pattern is waiting for you. After all pieces to be appliquéd have been cut, stay-stitched, and pressed, lay them down in their proper positions on the master pattern. Pin them to each other with a few pins to hold them together. When you are satisfied on positioning, transfer the pieces to your prepared background fabric. If you put a piece of cardboard underneath your work, it will be easier to pin the pieces onto the background material. Don't use too many pins. Place your pins vertical to a horizontal line of stitching (see Figure 14). Make certain all seams have their one-quarter inch overlap. Using an oval embroidery hoop, begin to stitch the pieces in place. **It is very important to work from the center of the figure outward.**

When doing appliqué, I only pin ahead of myself a few pins at a time as I turn under the seam allowance. See Figure 14 for correct pin placement in appliqué, binding, etc. Where there's a curve, simply clip up to the stay-stitch, not through it, before pinning. This makes turning under the one-quarter inch seam easier. Important: use the exact same thread color as the piece being sewn down when doing appliqué, and no more than about twelve inches long. The longer your thread, the more likely it will get tangled or caught in the pins, which is a waste of time. Use a normal sewing knot to begin your work and a double stitch underneath to secure it when the thread becomes too short and you need to fill your needle again. After I make a stitch, I give the thread a wee pull just to take any slack out of it. The stitches should be less than about a quarter inch in length and followed each time by my magic backstitch (see below).

Many quilters shy away from appliqué because they have been told it is difficult to hide the stitches. Not so. Hiding the stitch is easy. Unlike the usual appliqué stitch used to hem dresses, where the thread overlaps the hem top onto the background, my stitch doesn't overlap anything, because I sew straight through the appliqué to the background. The thread matches the appliqué material and shows only as a tiny dot on top of it.

Charlotte's Magic Backstitch

Using my backstitch technique will make it certain your stitches will not come out with wear and tear. This is the stitch I use to secure all my appliqué work and for binding off a quilt when it is completed. This stitch is totally invisible on appliqué and the final binding! It is easy and fast to do, too. Actually, the same type of stitch is used to set in a dress zipper.

Use Figure 15 as a guide. After each stitch, insert your needle just behind that same stitch. Appliqué and background are caught at the same time. Bring the needle through and up into the position for the next stitch. Repeat the procedure for each stitch you do. A tiny "dimple" on top of the appliqué, close to the edge, is all that will show.

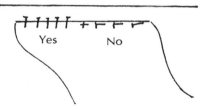

Figure 14. Pinning down appliqué or bias binding.

Putting on bias binding on the back of a quilt, using the backstitch.

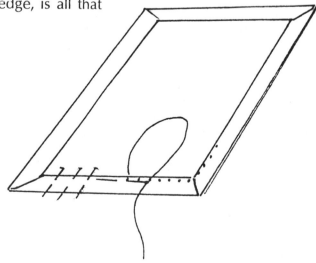

Figure 15. Binding off the back of a quilt using the backstitch.

Back cover of Indian Designs by David and Jean Villaseñor. I found and purchased this book soon after I began making Indian quilts. It has proved invaluable to me, as well as their Tapestries in Sand book, in my quest for patterns, ideas, symbols and design. (See Bibliography.)

Chapter 6

Tips on Background Layout and Design

Thou mystic thing, all beautiful!
What mind conceived thee, what intelligence began
And out of chaos thy rare shape designed,
Thou delicate and perfect work of man?

Thaxter

When appliqué is completed on the center piece of fabric, it is time to press it carefully. Next, measure its length and width to see if any distortion has occurred in its shape due to the appliqué (this often happens). Use a posterboard to check for squareness. If the background fabric is not square, trim it as necessary to square it up. Do not overtrim, as cut-off fabric can't be returned. Square corners are a must before sashing can be sewn on, binding placed, and for doing a mitred corner.

The Sashing

Sashing (side strips) should help accentuate the central appliquéd figure. Select colors for the sashing that are repeat colors of the main appliqué. Place the boldest color on the outside perimeter. This will give your work a framed look.

Your work may be completed without sashing. A simple bias binding is sufficient (see Chapter 9). But if you opt to do this, the background fabric for your appliqué should be larger...say about ten inches on the sides, bottom, and top.

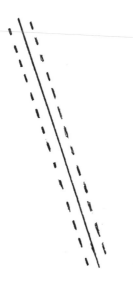

Figure 16. Reinforcing a machine stitch on sashing.

When I use sashing, I quilt one-quarter inch on both sides of the sashing's machine stitch to reinforce it (see Figure 16). This is especially important on regularly used quilts that undergo wear and tear. However, I do it on all my work. It used to be that the Amish insisted on this, but it is not seen too much anymore. I feel it is sloppy quilting if my "masterpieces" do not have those two extra lines, which add great design and character.

Below are six different quilt background layouts (see Figure 17). You can select one of these or create your own. Put a piece of tissue paper over the one you like best, trace it, and on that paper mark the width and length of the sashing. Use the measurements for your central piece first, then add on the measurements for the sides with sashing. It is perfectly acceptable to overlap the central image onto the sashing, as I have done. If you plan to do this, leave that part of the figure unsewn until it can be joined to the sashing when the sashing is attached to the background. This makes a wonderful point of interest. Everything doesn't have to be within a fixed perimeter.

Figure 17. Quilt background layouts.

After the sashing is cut, sew the strips together before stitching them to the central piece. For example, if you have two strips of different color side by side, sew these together first. I highly recommend taping a small, straight piece of cardboard on the needleplate of your sewing machine, one-half inch from the needle, to be used as a sewing guide. Allow half-inch seams on these strips, seams which should not be trimmed until all strips are sewn to the central piece. Note: I always add an extra inch to the length and width of the sashing as during sewing it might "draw up" and not fit to your main piece. Later on you can use the cardboard to square it off.

If you want to add an embellishing touch to your work with a bias insert or cording, now is the time to add them, **before** you sew the sashing to the central piece.

A Quick Bias Cutting Method

The great technique I have developed to save time cutting bias for inserts and binding (see Chapter 9) is illustrated in Figure 18. Try the system out by folding and cutting a newspaper first. You can cut the material for a bias insert and the material needed to bind the quilt (the bias binding) at the same time. I don't use fabric on the straight for finishing a quilt because it does not bend and roll. I also don't use the tube method of bias-making because by the time you have it all cut out and those little machine stitches begin to unravel, no time has been saved. What I do in my quick method is cut bias strips and then sew these strips together, backstitching them when I have them on the machine. There Is no need to cut long bias strips as in the "unfolded" method.

The Bias Insert

The bias insert is a narrow, folded strip of three-inch wide fabric sewn either to the edge of the sashing, or directly on the background material. It is sewn only on one side; the other side is allowed to flop and hang free. No more than one inch of insertion should "flop" on top of the quilt. "Bias" refers to a line diagonal to the grain of a fabric, especially a line at a 45° angle to the selvage. To emphasize my wolf image, I used a flat, three-inch wide piece of red, bias-cut fabric. (see Figure 19).

Prepare the bias insert as follows: (1) Cut as many three-inch wide pieces of bias as desired; fold lengthwise after they have been joined together; press. (2) Machine stitch the edge of the strip using about a half-inch seam. Press again. **Note:** It is imperative the bias be sewn together

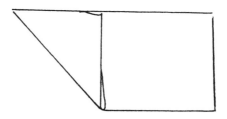

A. *Fold fabric from corner to corner at an angle to obtain bias. Cut with a sharp scissors. You will now have two triangles. Leave them in place.*

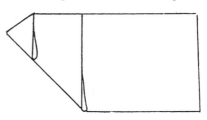

B. *Fold fabric again as shown, keeping the edges together.*

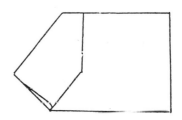

C. *Fold fabric over again, keeping the edges together.*

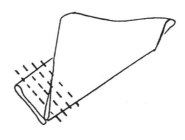

D. *The fabric is ready for cutting. Use your cardboard ruler to mark the width you want for bias. If the fold is uneven, adjust it before you cut.*

Figure 18. Folding fabric to cut bias the Charlotte Bass way!

first or it will creep out of shape when machine sewing it down. (3) Using your machine line stitch as a guide, attach the bias insert to sashing or background fabric. When sewing down to sashing, stitch on top of the stitching made when sewing the insert together. Press again. I have used this insert method on many of my works.

As mentioned earlier, I quilt about one-quarter inch on either side of a machine stitch where sashing is placed. When it comes to quilting the bias insert, however, it is only necessary to quilt on one side of the machine seam, because the insert acts as a reinforcement to the seam. By using the bias insert, I save time during quilting. I use the bias insert primarily for wall hangings, not for bed quilts.

Making Cording

Another exciting embellishment that is fun to make is cording. It is used to repeat a color next to a piece of sashing or it is used alone. Regular cording, thin upholstery cording, or butcher string all work well. I add cording to my quilted wall hangings but never to my bed quilts, since cording shrinks and bed quilts are more likely to need washing.

To make cording, take a solid piece of fabric, preferably bias cut, and lay the cording on the material (see Figure 20). Lap the fabric over the cording about two inches (more or less, depending on how thick your cording is), and use the sewing machine's zipper foot to stitch the fabric down as close as you can get it to the cording. Use matching color thread as sometimes the thread might show when sewing the cording onto the sashing. When you get to the end of the fabric, cut the fabric to the left of the stitching line (with the cording on the right), leaving a one-half inch seam allowance. Move the cording just covered to the top of the fabric section you just cut off. Fold the fabric back about half an inch to avoid a raw seam on your completed cording; then repeat the process until you have all the cording you need.

When you get the rhythm of making cording, you'll wonder how you ever lived without it. If you really want to get fancy, you can make double cording. With the zipper foot in place, finish the first cording and then add the second cording (which should be thinner than the first) on top of the first cording. If you do this, make the first cording seam allowance a little wider than a half-inch.

Using cording saves even more time than using the bias insert because there are no bias strips to cut out and no

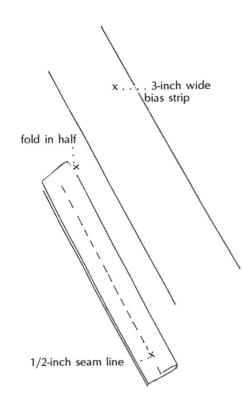

x . . . . 3-inch wide
bias strip

fold in half

1/2-inch seam line

Figure 19. Making a folded bias insert.

sewing those strips together. It does, however, have a tendency to "draw up" the work, so you have to use a large stitch for control, and you must pull the cording and fabric through the sewing machine. Cording should be placed in the same area where the bias insert would go if you were using it and stitched down in exactly the same manner. In other words, stitch it to the sashing or to the center piece on the same seam line that you used to cover the cording.

When cordings meet at a corner, instead of sewing one over the other, pull out about half an inch of each cording and clip it off, leaving the coverings. This prevents excessive thickness when you sew the two pieces over each other, and the seams will then lay flat. After making cording, it is a good idea to smooth it down with your hand to ease out any pulling that might have occurred.

Cutting and Trimming Excess Fabric

After your sashing work is complete, follow these steps prior to the final pressing of the quilt top:

Look at your appliqué figure on the front. Do you see any discoloration because two or more colors have overlapped each other? For example, a piece of yellow over a dark green background fabric results in a mud color. If so, you need to cut out the excess fabric that is causing the discoloration. Cutting and trimming are done on the underside of your quilt top. This includes the main back piece upon which your Indian figure is sewn. After that is removed, then some of the smaller pieces which have overlapping can be cut or trimmed. *When cutting, always leave a one-quarter inch seam allowance.* Use a small pair of scissors and take care not to clip too much. The purity of color you attain by cutting out all the excess will make the effort well worth while.

After this, trim the sashing and center piece seams to one-quarter inch also. Lastly, with your finger, open the seams on the backside of the quilt top and press them flat with an iron. Also press the appliqué work. Use a towel underneath on an ironing board for a nice even press.

Another way to compensate for a mud color is to do some stuffing, or "trapunto." For example, to improve facial color, I place a bright red piece of fabric under the cheeks before appliqué is done. Just a small round patch does wonders. On other works you might consider doing this with the hands also. Rosy looks are happy and they give more energy to the subject.

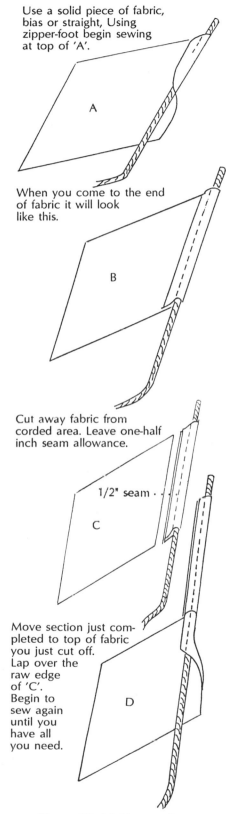

Use a solid piece of fabric, bias or straight, Using zipper-foot begin sewing at top of 'A'.

A

When you come to the end of fabric it will look like this.

B

Cut away fabric from corded area. Leave one-half inch seam allowance.

1/2" seam

C

Move section just completed to top of fabric you just cut off. Lap over the raw edge of 'C'. Begin to sew again until you have all you need.

D

Figure 20. Making cording.

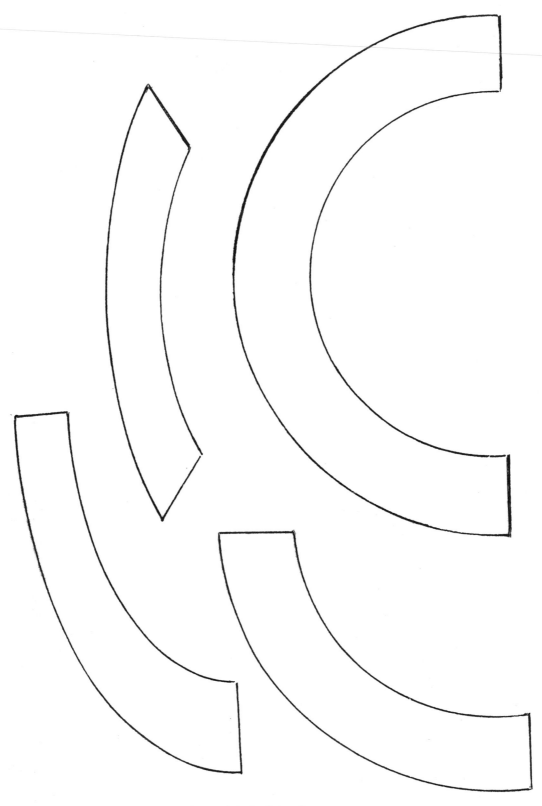

Figure 21. Quilting line patterns.

Crow Mother with many innovations including authentic beads, and a real woven basket with fabric stuffed corn.
From the collection of Dr. and Mrs. Darshan Mahajan

KERWAN, The Bean Dancer - Hopi *celebrates purification and renovation of the earth for future planting.*

Late 19th century lodgemaker - Arapaho*, burns sage and dances about new tipis and lodges to drive away evil spirits and purify all.*

MOMO, The Bee Kachina - Zuni *imitates the hum of the bee and shoots tiny arrows as bee stings at misbehaving childrens legs; if the cry, gives them honey*

HUMIS "Hemis Kachina" *is principal character in Niman Kachina "Home Dance", the last dance of the year when all Kachinas go home.*

Chapter 7:
The Simple Truth About Quilting

How happy is he born and taught
That serveth not another's will,
Whose armor is his honest thought,
And simple truth his utmost skill!

Sir Henry Wotten, "A Happy Life"

The time is now ready to put your work on a frame or in a hoop and quilt. To quilt means to put a design on your quilt top, by drawing on quilting lines, and then to stitch the three layers of material called the "sandwich" together. The sandwich consists of the quilt back, the interior batting, and the quilt top. The quilt back is always cut two inches longer and wider than the batting, and the quilt top is always two inches shorter in width and length than the batting. *Never have all three pieces cut even with each other.* If your work shifts, you can't add on material to make up for it! Quilting is like basting. Basting is stitching loosely with long stitches, and quilting is stitching loosely with short stitches. Simple!

Pencil Quilting Lines

Use a regular wooden lead pencil to mark your quilting lines on both the background layout and the central image. The lines will disappear in the quilting if they are not too dark (see Figure 11). Indian symbols which have been enlarged can be used for design. I usually use pieces of posterboard cut into various shapes and lengths to draw on designs. In Figure 21 you will find some examples of quilting line patterns, which you can increase in size to the length and width you need. Use straight cuttings to draw lines on the bias, sashing, or

41

MY QUILTING TECHNIQUE ILLUSTRATED

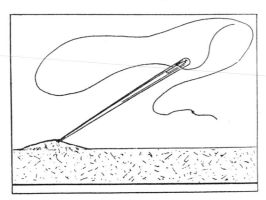

Figure 22a. Hand tie a simple knot at the end of the quilting thread. Without wearing a thimble, put the threaded needle through the top layer of the quilt only.

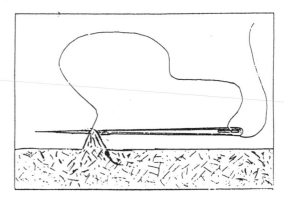

Figure 22b. Bring out the needle, and in the same hole pick up a few top fibers with the needle to secure the knot. Be careful not to pull too hard at first as the little knot may come through the fabric.

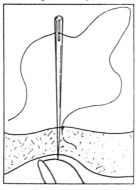

Figure 22c. Put on your thimble. Start the first stitch by pointing the needle straight down and pushing gently until you barely feel the needle on your finger underneath. If the needle doesn't go straight down, your first and subsequent stitches will be too long.

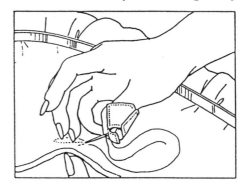

Figure 22d. Bend the needle and direct it back upward through the "hill" you make by pushing up the bottom fabric with your finger underneath. When the needle passes through the top layer, immediately aim it down again.

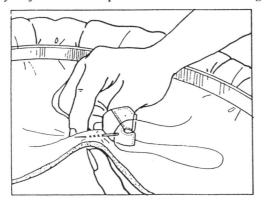

Figure 22e. When you have three stitches on the needle (three is enough to begin with), squeeze the fabric and push the needle through with your thimble. Making a valley with your finger underneath will help.

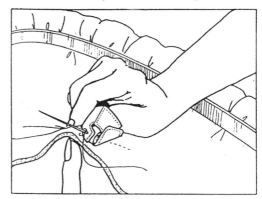

Figure 22f. Don't use up your thread to the last inch or two. Leave enough thread to knot off the last stitch. To secure the last stitch, bring the needle out and slip a couple of stitches on the top fabric only, picking up just a few threads (same as step no. 2).

central piece. Whatever the width of your sashing, divide it in half and draw a straight line in the middle for the quilting line. The distance between your quilting lines should be proportionate with the lines you draw on the central figure. If the widest unquilted part of the figure is about one inch wide, then the balance of the quilt should incorporate similar measurements. Having some lines too close and others too far apart will make your piece look out of balance.

Quilting lines are used to add texture to the appliqué figure. Should it need a muscle line in the arm or leg, put one there. The neck may also need help. Perhaps add a few extra lines in the tunic or clout to make them look real. Don't hesitate to add lines where you think they will improve the appearance of your work.

Charlotte's Quick Quilting Technique

It is said about writing with an old-fashioned fountain pen, "use your own, as each hand has its own pressure." If you have never heard this phrase, it is an old timer. The same principle applies to the quilting techniques you develop. Use the techniques that work best for you. But because my quilting technique, which I developed over a number of years, is fast, you will find it worth learning. I do not hold my needle, but put in about 5–7 stitches at once on a straight line (three on a curve) using only the pressure of the needle leaned against my thimble and the quilt. I start by planting the needle straight down, make a valley, and then push the needle back up. I continue with a rolling or wiggling motion to put in stitches until the needle is full. Then I squeeze the quilt, push the needle through with the thimble, pull gently, and start the next movement. By not holding the needle, but laying it into the thimble, no fingers get in the way. The pressure between the thimble (on either my thumb or middle finger) and my hand under the quilt is the secret. Keeping the quilt loose in the hoop or floor frame allows the needle to slide through quickly. (Most quilters keep their quilts too taut.) There should be just enough dimple in the quilt that it jiggles up and down when shaken.

When I begin again, I follow the same steps, except that I start one stitch behind where I ended. This way the tiny stitches to begin and end are less noticeable on top of the quilt. Do not work with a thread too long or too short. About sixteen inches is just right. In the beginning, if on a straight line pattern, try to get about three stitches on the needle. After you develop your own rhythm, try to get five to seven stitches on the needle.

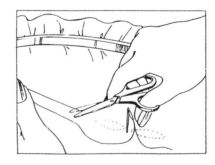

Figure 22g. Lastly, run your needle full length between the sandwich, leaving about an inch of thread inside, and cut the thread where the needle comes out.

On a curve, three stitches are maximum. These figures are for using Fatt Batt. Expect more stitches if using regular weight batting. Lastly, remember that the hills and valleys you make with your fingers underneath as you quilt make all the difference.

The Size of Quilting Stitches

A word about quilting stitches. Don't spend a lot of time worrying about how long or short they are, or how they look on the backside of your work. Life is too short! You will get the hang of getting them the right size with time. Just try to make your stitches even, and complete your work. When using Fatt Batt, I average seven stitches to the inch. When using a thinner batting, I have about eight or nine stitches per inch. This is my rhythm. You might get more or less. Remember the fountain pen analogy at the beginning of this chapter.

Quilting with a Floor Frame

I have quilted major works on a floor frame in a week using my quick quilting method. See Figure 23, where the threads look like they are floating. I work as far as my left arm will allow me to travel underneath, then leave the needle and thread in the quilt and go to the next area. I sometimes have twenty-five to thirty needles going in the quilt at a time. After quilting with the last needle, I roll the quilt toward me and go back to continue with the first needle.

When using a floor frame, always begin your quilting at the bottom middle, because if you goof, your mistake can be hidden behind a pillow. Go clear across the bottom with quilting stitches, then go back to the center and work to the right or left as the pattern demands. This method will prevent you from having a crooked quilt. If your needle gets sticky during the work, rub it through your hair, or rub your finger behind your ear and rub the body oil on your needle, or have a piece of waxed paper nearby and stab your needle through it as often as needed.

Before turning the quilt roller, but after you have completed as much as possible, be certain to baste up the sides of the quilt and pull the thread to match the pull on your quilt stitches. By doing this you will completely avoid having a work with wavy sides. When the work is finished, do the same thing at the top and bottom of the quilt to assure straightness.

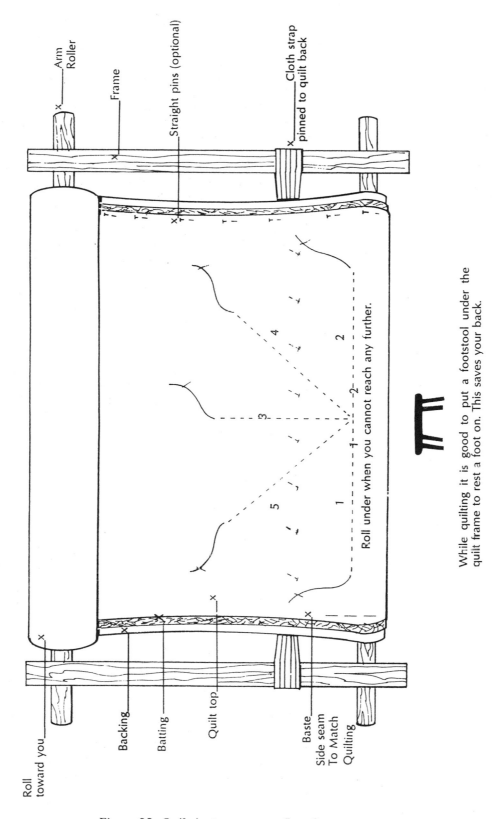

Arm
Roller

Frame

Straight pins (optional)

Cloth strap
pinned to quilt back

Roll
toward you

Backing

Batting

Quilt top

Baste
Side seam
To Match
Quilting

Roll under when you cannot reach any further.

While quilting it is good to put a footstool under the
quilt frame to rest a foot on. This saves your back.

Figure 23. Quilt in process on a floor frame.

Quilting with a Hoop

When quilting with a hoop, always begin at the center of your work and move gradually outward in an around-and-around pattern. Continue to move around the circumference of your quilting, as indicated in Figure 24, until the work is completed. If you don't, your work won't look right or won't hang right.

Since the hoop is moved around and around, I do not leave needles in the fabric when using a hoop. I leave the threads hanging loose and pick them up again with the needle as I move the hoop. The only interference encountered while turning the hoop is the brass safety pins used to hold the sandwich together. I use brass safety pins because they don't rust.

When coming close to the edge, you can add an extra piece of fabric with pins or basting to extend the edge. This will give your hoop something to grab onto so you can finish the pattern. There is no need to purchase a half-circle hoop to finish. As you move the quilt around, the safety pins will have to be moved every now and then. This releases the back tension. Do not have your fabric pulled too tightly. Leave a "poof" in the center so you can roll your needle for speed. When done, add a basting stitch one-half inch in from the edge all the way around. This compensates for quilt stitch pull.

Cutting and Trimming

When you are done quilting on the hoop or floor frame, trim off excess backing and batting with a large, sharp pair of scissors. Use your posterboard to check the squareness of the corners and place it along the cutting line when cutting to ensure straightness. Remember to have all four sides "pulled up" to match quilting tightness by using a large basting stitch. This prevents "ocean wave" sides. Now the work is ready for hanging sleeves or straps and the finishing bias binding.

Counterpane or Wholecloth Quilting

Counterpane or wholecloth quilting means using one solid piece of fabric. Through the magic of your own fingers you can create your Indian quilt without doing any appliqué if you wish. To use this method, prepare your master pattern as suggested, but instead of using pieces of different colored fabric, simply place the paper pattern beneath the background fabric (a light color so you can see the pattern beneath it), and trace on the pattern.

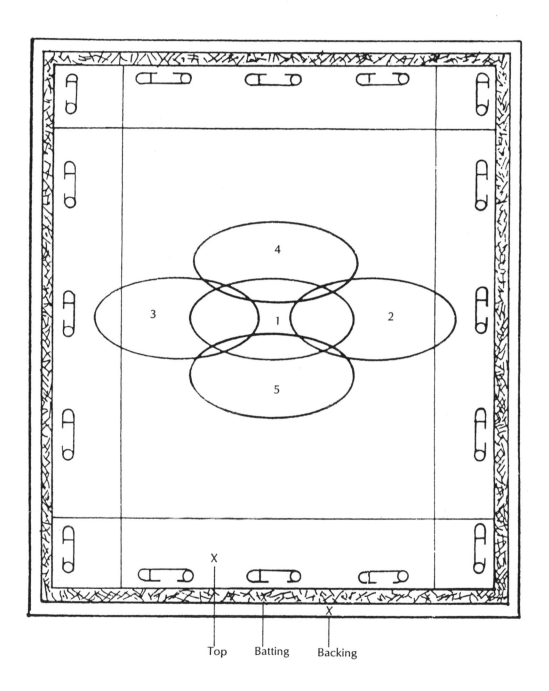

Figure 24. Quilting in an around-and-around pattern in a hoop.

Side sashing may be added if you desire. A plain work is beautiful as well.

Finding a Quilting Teacher

If you want to find a quilting teacher, try to find a knowledgeable quilting teacher who is willing to teach you quilting first. I don't recommend learning to piece first. That is not quilting. Piecing is cutting out tiny pieces of fabric, usually from expensive material, then sewing them together to make a pattern. Trying to get the points of material to match is usually tedious and frustrating. Your quilting teacher should teach you how to quilt: to put a design on a fabric and then stitch the three layers of the sandwich together. This is quilting. Unfortunately, most teachers do not teach quilting to beginners. They usually teach piecing first, then quilting, and rarely appliqué. They should teach appliqué after quilting and save piecing for the last step.

First-time quilters often like to start with something small such as a doll quilt to keep in the family. Never give away your first work. Refer back to it as a yardstick for measuring improvement on your next quilts.

Chapter 8:
Adding Hanging Sleeves or Straps

That is the usual method, but not mine—
My way is to begin from the beginning;
The regularity of my design
Forbids all wandering as the worst of sinning.

Edmund Spencer from Don Juan, 1918

Making a smaller work hang beautifully is difficult. I have found that by adding sleeves at the top and bottom of a work, it hangs better. In the case of using straps on the top, it is necessary to put a sleeve on the bottom. The rods and newells (end decorations), which are inserted in the sleeves, look professional on all work!

Hanging Sleeves

The method is simple:

1. Use the same fabric you used for the backing. Measure the top and bottom of the quilt to see if both are the same width. If not, you will have to adjust your quilted wall tapestry by pulling those "ocean-wave" basting threads you carefully applied, and secure them. If this doesn't work, lay the quilt flat on a table and hand push it around. If the measure is still unequal, you will have to use posterboard to obtain a square corner, and you might have to trim. Be very careful if you trim, as you can never return the trimmed material.

2. If all is now even (top and bottom should be equal measurements), add two inches each for the top and bottom. Cut two strips this length by nine inches wide.

3. Turn under one inch at one end of the material for a smooth finish, and press. Then fold the nine-inch-wide

piece of fabric in half lengthwise and press. Stay-stitch, using matching thread, about one-half inch from the bottom edge to within five inches of the edge not folded under. This will allow space for adjustment when the casing is attached to the quilt (see Figure 25). Repeat this process with the second piece of fabric.

4. Pin the finished side of each sleeve on the quilt (one at the top and one at the bottom) at least one-half inch in from the side margin to leave room for the bias binding. With a wide machine stitch sew the casing in place. When you get close to the end of the sleeve, there should be extra fabric left. Ascertain how much has to be cut off, allowing one inch for turning under as you did at the beginning, and leaving one-half inch of space for the bias binding at the end. Cut the material and finish machine stitching the sleeves down. All of this is like making an old fashioned header casing for a fine window curtain.

5. When adding the bias binding (see Chapter 9), take care not to stitch down the opening of the sleeve casing. Hand stitch the sleeve (the flapping edge) in place. The casing should be about four inches down from the seam top and four inches up from the seam bottom. Pinning vertical to a horizontal line will make your work go faster (see Figure 14).

Hanging Straps

The tube-casing method is the one usually used by most quilters. However, I feel straps add elegance to a work and take it out of the "ordinary" and place it into the "extraordinary" category. Here is the method:

1. Measure the quilt top to make sure it is even and squared off (see sleeve information above). Subtract one inch for the two half-inch bias bindings on the sides, as the straps will be sewn on the area between the two bias bindings. Using this measurement, decide how many straps you need, placing straps between five and seven inches apart. To begin, place one at each side of the work one-half inch in from where the bias binding will be sewn. Place one dead center, and work out from there. If you want, you can cut newspaper dummies to the size (length and width) you like and place them on your quilt to see how many straps you need for a nice presentation.

2. Measure the strap length desired and double it. Add one more inch to allow a half-inch on each end to stitch the strap to the quilt. For example, if you want a five by

Press down 1-inch on open sleeve.

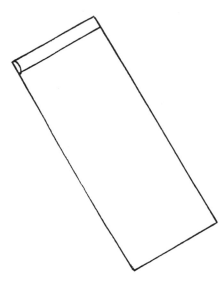

Fold in half lengthwise and press. Stay-stitch about 1/2 inch on bottom leaving end open about 5 inches. Press.

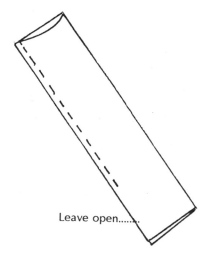

Leave open......

Figure 25. Making a sleeve casing.

four inch strap, the cut should be eleven inches long by nine inches wide.

3. With the measurements complete, cut your fabric. I prefer cutting on the "straight" of the fabric, as the straps hang better.

4. Stitch a half-inch seam on each strap, and then trim the seams to one-quarter inch. Gently press open the seam allowance with your fingers, center the seam in the middle, turn the strap right-side out, and press (see Figure 26). Stay stitch across the bottoms using a half-inch seam. Press the seam line.

5. When all the straps are complete, space them equally on your quilt (as laid out in step number one above) and pin in place.

6. Machine sew the straps on the *front side* of your work, not on the backside. The seam should be just short of a half-inch (see Figure 27). At this point, you are ready to sew on your bias binding (see next chapter).

7. After the bias binding is all sewn down (see Figure 28), add the stuffing if you wish for a professional touch. It is time to tack the front side of the straps to the bias binding with a few stitches (see Figure 29); otherwise, the quilt will not hang correctly.

A. *Hanging strap strip cut on straight of fabric.*

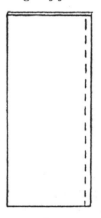

B. *Half-inch seam allowance trimmed to one-quarter inch.*

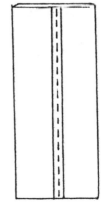

C. *Seam allowance centered and finger pressed open.*

Figure 26. Preparing hanging straps.

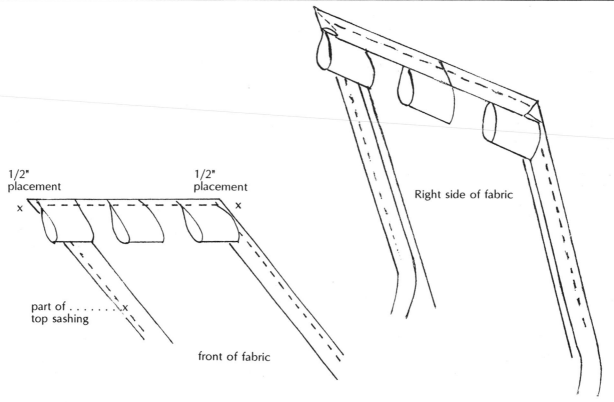

1/2"
placement

1/2"
placement

x   x

part of x
top sashing

front of fabric

Right side of fabric

Figure 27. Sewing on straps. Be sure to
leave one-half inch open on each edge where
straps will be placed

Figure 28. Sewing on the bias binding; bias ends
top center.

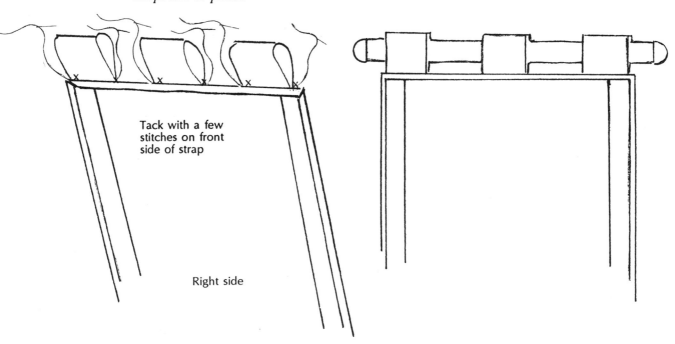

Tack with a few
stitches on front
side of strap

Right side

Figure 29. Finishing the hanging straps.
Tack straps to finished binding where loose
threads are shown.

Figure 30. Quilted tapestry hanging from straps.

Chapter 9:
Bias Binding, Mitred Corners, and Final Embellishments

Not enjoyment, and not sorrow,
Is our destined end or way;
But to act, that each tomorrow
Find us farther than today!

Longfellow, A Psalm of Life

The bias binding is a narrow strip of bias-cut fabric that wraps around and binds off the edges of your quilt to protect it from fraying. "Bias" refers to a line diagonal to the grain of the fabric; i.e. a line diagonal to the selvage (the tight woven edge of material). Cut the fabric for the bias binding as illustrated in Figure 19, sew the pieces together, and press open the seams. You should have one solid piece of bias for binding the whole quilt. When using Fatt Batt to stuff my bias binding, which is most of the time, I cut the bias two-and-a-half inches wide. I sew it onto the quilt with a half-inch seam. It rolls beautifully, even with seam stuffing. If you are using a thinner batt, cut your bias just shy of two inches wide. A marked cardboard "ruler" works well to mark the bias for cutting. I keep several posterboard rulers marked for various sizes.

Sewing Down the Binding

Start by machine stitching the finishing binding using a half-inch seam, the right side to the quilt top.[2] The binding should be able to wrap around an equal distance on

---

2 Before proceeding with the binding, study the next section on mitred corners as well.

Imaginary or real dot at
half-inch intersection.

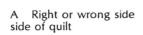

A   Right or wrong side
side of quilt

the opposite side of the quilt plus enough fabric to fold under and handstitch in place. Use a medium stitch and sew slowly, finger-pressing the three layers of the quilt plus bias binding carefully just before they move under the machine needle. Try to follow the wide basting stitch at the quilt edge as a machine stitching guide. Begin the machine stitch at the top-middle of your quilted wall tapestry, leaving about a four-inch tail unsewn. When you get around to the top again, stop about five inches from where you began, again leaving about a four-inch tail. Remove the quilt from the sewing machine. Lap the two tail ends over each other. In the center of one (about two inches from where you began the stitch), cut it off at a 45° angle. Then lap the other tail over the one you just cut, and cut it at an opposite angle so that the two ends will fit together perfectly. But cut the last piece so that it overlaps the first piece by one-half inch. The half inch is so that when you sew the pieces together, you will have a one-quarter inch seam. Now hold the two pieces of bias, or pin them, and return to the machine to stitch them together. There is no need to iron them; you can use your fingers. Lastly, lay the connected bias on your quilt and finish stitching it across (see Figure 28). The binding on the top, or front, of your quilt is now complete.

About a Mitred Corner

It is absolutely necessary to have a perfectly square corner for great mitred results with this technique. Sewing your bias binding down on the front side of your quilt will take you to four corners. When you come to the first one, and instructions are the same for the other three, follow these steps:

1. Remember to always maintain a half-inch seam. When you approach the corner, before you arrive, stick a straight pin in at the half-inch mark (half an inch in from both sides of the corner).

2. Stitch to that point, backstitch, and then remove the quilt from the machine and the pin from the quilt.

3. Fold the bias into a tent, with the machine stitch helping you make the tent. Be certain the fold is flush to the top of your quilt (see Figure 31).

4. Put in a straight pin from the back where the last stitch shows and have it come through to the side where you will be stitching. Return the quilt to the sewing machine, plant your needle exactly where the pin is located,

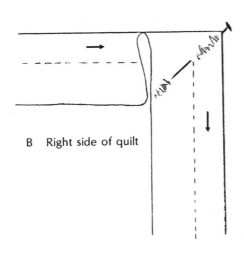

B   Right side of quilt

Make mitre corner tent,
bring straight pin up
from back, put in
machine needle and go.

Figure 31. Mitre corner tent.

forward and backstitch 3–4 stitches, remove the pin, and take the journey to the next corner.

After all four corners of your work have been mitred, it is time to turn the bias under about one-half inch (binding the quilt edges) and stitch it to the quilt back with my backstitch (the same one you used for appliqué). Follow these steps.

1. When you come to a mitred corner, stop finishing the binding about three inches before and three inches after it. Never try to "just go around it" with your stitches. This is impossible.

2. With your straight pins, pin the bias down to each corner, carefully rolling it in place...perhaps a wiggle will help.

3. If you have trouble with the mitre making too much of a point, readjust your bias. It is essential that you have perfectly square corners on your quilt to make this work.

4. I never put a stitch on the front side of a mitred corner, just one small "tack" stitch on the backside. It is more beautiful being plain.

5. When sewing down the binding, lap it over the machine stitches you used to put the binding on the front. This will give a neater finish.

6. If you are using stuffing under your binding, stop short of the mitre area and do not put any in there.

Stuffing the Bias Binding

Stuffing the bias binding is optional, but if you do it, your work will have a stronger finish, an extra bit of class. I like to stuff the inside of my bias binding, next to the outside of the quilt, with ever so little batting. I usually use leftover batting trimmed from the quilt. I stretch it a bit to thin it out. The total bias stuffing shouldn't be more than a pencil width thick. Be careful not to stuff mitred corners.

Embellishments Take Imagination

Only after the work is completed should the embellishments be added. Use your imagination; make them exciting. You should have been thinking about what to use long before now. Perhaps you have a collection of things from which to select. Gathering "things" for adding charm is important. I frequently attach black-tipped, white turkey feathers, representing eagle feathers, to my work. Feathers, depending on how they were worn or cut, symbolized different things to the Plains Indians.

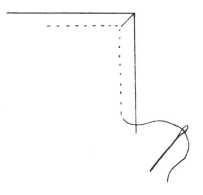

Figure 32. The back of a quilt with a mitred corner. These stitches are about one-quarter inch apart.

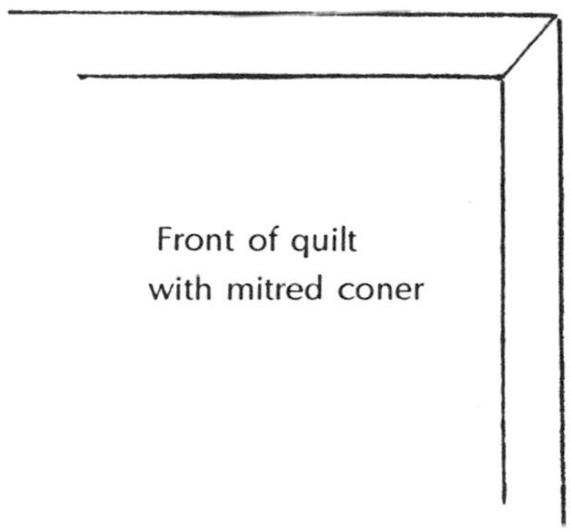

Front of quilt with mitred coner

Figure 33. The front of a quilt with a mitred corner.

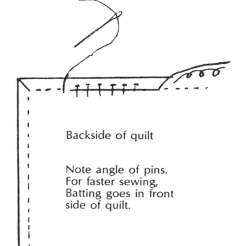

Backside of quilt

Note angle of pins. For faster sewing, Batting goes in front side of quilt.

Figure 34. Stuffing the inside of the bias binding.

Also, consider using brightly colored chicken feathers, artificial flowers, leaves, beads, fringe, cactus designs, and so forth. Be daring—but be careful not to make your quilted wall tapestry appear too busy.

If there is a powwow or Indian festival in your area, you will probably find vendors selling authentic Native American materials at reasonable prices. Such events are wonderful sources for items to attach to your work at one time or another. Instead of wearing bells some dancers sew on cone-shaped tin snuff box tops. Other items you may find include deer toes, shells, tassels, animal heads or bones, skins, horsetails, bead work, loose beads of all sizes, antlers, porcupine quills, various buttons, and beautiful stones. Ribbons and yarns are also popular decoration items.

If you want to add leather fringe, the technique to make your own is quite simple. Take a clean, soft piece of deer hide and moisten it well with water. Then cut it in thin strips from the outer edge toward the center. One small piece of leather makes a great deal of fringe.

KACHINA NECK RUFFS (collars): Many kachinas have ruffs around their necks made from fur, feathers, fabric, or skins. They hide shoulder braces required to carry heavy ceremonial headpieces. Making a kachina ruff is fun. After all body appliqué is completed, including a flat ruff, I add the three dimensional ruff to be stuffed.

You can give dimension to a ruff by stuffing it with batting. Measure the length of the neck collar, and double that measurement in length. Add about two inches to the width of the ruff to allow for the small amount of batting that will be placed inside. To obtain the right amount of batting, I tell my students to take what they think is necessary for a stuffing, then put half of it back. That is my formula for all stuffing and trapunto. Allowing the usual one-quarter inch seam allowance, handstitch the ruff top and corners to the kachina's neck leaving about two inches open. Then insert the batting, pin the bottom closed, and continue sewing to finish it. I often add embellishments to a ruff. Beads, embroidery, feathers, torn fabrics with frayed edges, fur, or a few handstitches to make puffs here and there. Anything to complement the design is fun. Use your imagination.

HAKTO, Man Who Carries Wood on His Head - Zuni. *Antlers and horns are hit together to sound like deer or elk are fighting.*

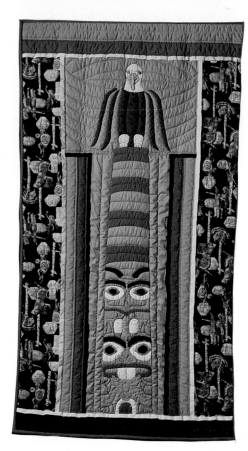

Heraldic Column, The Totem Pole - Haida. *Beautiful carvings of family history, with animals representing family clans, are placed in front of their lodges.*

Navajo Yei *holding lightning strikes which signify the need for rain. Medicine bag holds charms and seeds.*

MONGWA, The Great Horned Owl - Hopi, *dances in mixed Kachina festivals and dances on 1st, 2nd and 3rd Mesas.*

KWEO, The Wolf Kachina - Hopi, *hides behind his staff (representing a tree), so he can spring to quick action.
From the collection of Lawrence and Susan Fox, Highland Park Il.*

Chapter 10:
Patterns to Please You

Make Wisdom, too, your own:
If you find it, you may look forward to the future,
And your thread of life will not be cut short. — Proverbs 24:14

Patterns are everywhere, and in this chapter I have included many to tickle your fancy. All of these designs can be used to decorate both wall hangings and regular utility quilts, whether in appliqué or wholecloth. Remember, capturing a dream with your needle and thread can last forever. When you have started your first quilt utilizing Southwest Indian designs, think about the above proverb. Your work will be a constant reminder of the love and toil that went into it. Take no criticism about your stitches or your ideas. Just do your own thing, whatever it might be.

A Word of Cheer
Because I heard a word of praise,
I found new pleasure in my task,
And profit which in former days
Had seemed too great for me to ask,
Because I heard a word of cheer
The way that had been rough before,
Became a pleasant way and clear,
Where small things daunted me no more.

How to Make a Wolf-Kachina Appliquéd Wall Hanging

For a subject to lead you through step by step, I have chosen a wolf kachina pattern. The Hopi revere the wolf kachina, *Kweo* or *Kwewu*, as a deity of survival. Artist, Donna Greenlee describes this kachina's appearance:

The wolf kachina wears a brown case mask with red and black eyes. He has a snout with teeth and black wolf tracks are painted on his cheeks. He wears a fox skin ruff, a breech clout, red horsehair skirt, a blue-green belt, and red moccasins. Kweo's body is painted yellow on the back and white on the front. His forearms and lower legs are painted black with white spots. He is seen leaning on a cane. Kweo appears in a mixed kachina dance and water serpent ceremony at First Mesa.[3]

3   A mesa is a flat topped rocky hill with steeply sloping sides on which many Indians in the Southwest make their homes. First Mesa, Second Mesa, Third Mesa, etc. are home territory designations.

During my research, I found different colors designated for the wolf's body, and I took artistic license to make some changes. "Authorities" disagree on colors, which makes it easier to bend the "rules." It is now time to make a list of colors as *you* see them and decide where you want them located. This is called plotting a course or making a recipe chart. Next, mark your appliqué patterns with the color codes you have selected: a number for each color, as in Figure 35. By doing this you will have a better idea of the amount of each fabric you need. Check your scrap bag first, though, to avoid making unnecessary purchases.

WOLF QUILT COLOR CHART

1. Brown — wolf body
2. Teal — belt, armbands, pole; top, bottom, and side strips
3. Gray — fur ruff around the neck
4. Tan — moccasins, shoulder straps, ear inset; side strips
5. White — feathers, clout (kilt skirt), hands, teeth, moccasin soles, cuffs on arm sleeves and leggings
6. Black — eyes, cheek paw marks, appliqué on clout; background, back of quilt, two casings for quilt back
7. Red — eye circles, red-stained horse-hair skirt, inside of mouth, feathers on cane; side strip and binding
8. Orange — underlining for the moon
9. Gold lamé — moon
10. Polka dots — (black and white) arm and leg coverings
11. Wolf print — wolf head (or make the head tan or brown); side strips
12. Tan fringe — moccasin tops, ties on cane

Figure 35. Color coding the wolf pattern.

The wolf-print fabric which I used for the head was also used for side sashing in the background layout. Since this fabric has gold-tipping, I added a gold moon to the quilted tapestry for the fellow to howl by! I purchased the fabric months before I even thought about doing the wolf, as it was so interesting.

Use for quilt line

X

X - - - - - - For Wolf face

Figure 36. Bear paw-mark. This is the actual size of the bear paw-mark used at the bottom of my tapestry. The small paw-mark can be used to decorate the face of the wolf.

WOLF QUILT YARDAGE REQUIREMENTS

Your own closet may yield the fabrics you need to make the wolf quilt. If not, here is a complete list of the yardage requirements for the colors and pieces specified above using 44–45-inch-wide fabrics. In regard to my fabric quantities, I never piece together any side strips, as it looks better to have a continuous piece. The wolf is about 36 inches tall.

Brown	⅔ yard
Teal	1½ yards
Gray	¼ yard
Tan	½ yard (2 yards if using tan for the wolf head and side strips)
White	½ yard
Black	3½ yards
Red	2 yards
Orange	⅔ yard
Gold Lamé	⅔ yard
Polka dots	⅓ yard
Wolf print	1½ yards
Tan fringe	⅓ yard
Black floss	1 skein (for embroidery)

Matching thread (for fabric stay-stitching and appliqué)

STAY-STITCHING AND PATTERN LAYOUT ON THE STRAIGHT OF FABRIC

Your fabrics and colors have been chosen, and the paper pattern pieces have been cut out. It is time to lay the individual paper pieces on the various fabric colors and pin them carefully in place, on the straight of material as much as possible (see Figure 37). The fabric pieces will handle better after they are cut this way.

Outline each piece on the fabric with a no. 2 pencil. Do not press too hard; keep your lines light. Be certain to leave space around each piece for a one-quarter inch seam allowance for turning under when you do appliqué.

Remove the paper patterns, and using a matching thread and a medium stitch, stay-stitch or hand embroider (using a hoop) on the penciled lines. This makes finger-turning the pieces easier to do when sewing them down.

Next, cut out the pieces of fabric. For this project life will be sweeter by stay-stitching as much as possible in a solid piece, and then press before cutting out the pieces.

Using a machine stay-stitch often causes the fabric to pucker. To avoid this, clip a bobbin stitch with your ripper wherever the material is pulling. Don't clip too often, though, as it may cancel your stitching. Iron press the pieces on the backside to flatten them and take out some of the pucker.

Note: If you opt to hand embroider your work, this is done before cutting out the individual pieces. I use two (out of six) strands of black embroidery floss to emphasize certain parts of the subject, although a simple quilting line would suffice. It's your choice.

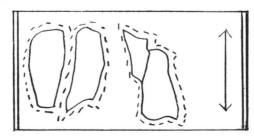

Figure 37. Laying out wolf pattern pieces on fabric.

MAKING THE WOLF'S HEAD, TEETH, AND TONGUE

1. Cut the wolf's head in the manner explained as one solid piece of material (see Figure 38). Note that the gray ruff will be used for the back of the wolf's head.

2. Using your master pattern as a guide, embroider or machine stay-stitch the mouthline so that the mouth appears to be open (see Figure 35). Press the back side of the material, but do not cut it.

3. Cut a piece of white fabric for the teeth after outlining the teeth with black single strand floss.

4. Appliqué the teeth onto a piece of bright red fabric which you have cut to fit inside the mouthline. The tongue of the mouth should hang down and be embroidered with single strand black floss.

5. Now cut out the area inside the mouthline on the head, leaving a one-quarter inch margin for the seam. Place the red mouth with its tongue and teeth on the area you have just cut out, and stitch it down with matching thread. Add a few rhinestones to look like saliva. Use reverse appliqué (see Chapter 5) to attach the inner ear.

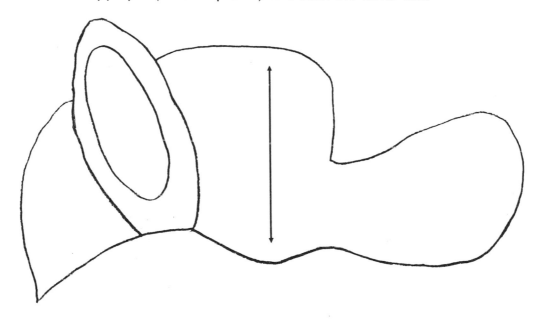

Figure 38. Outline of the wolf's head.

MAKING THE REST OF THE WOLF FIGURE

Continue to use the uncut master pattern to lay all the pieces in their proper places. Remember to always leave enough seam overlap (at least one-quarter inch) so that you have something to sew one piece on to another. Pin each piece in place, placing the pins sideways to the seam, not lengthwise (see Figure 14). Don't use too many pins. Some of the pieces, like the wolf's head above, may require preliminary appliqué of subordinate pieces before pinning the larger piece to the background material.

I chose gray for the fur ruff around the neck. If you happen to have a real piece of fur, use it; or cut some gray fabric, shred the ends, and hand appliqué this on after the quilting is completed. I decided to add definition embroidery (using two strands of floss) to miscellaneous lines on the wolf's collar for more drama. I made the entire body brown from the shoulders to the knees, and drew some muscle lines on the body pattern as too much unquilted space looks terrible.

WOLF BACKGROUND FABRIC, SASHING, AND QUILT BACK

A black background for the wolf to rest upon was my choice after trying several other colors. It made a more dynamic statement. I also chose black for the backing of this quilt and the sleeves because black doesn't show dirt. (See Chapter 8 on how to make top and bottom sleeves.) I never use a printed fabric on the back of a quilted wall tapestry because I like to see my quilting stitches. Why hide that work?

The size of the sashing (or stripping) pieces, which are sewn to the background fabric of the central figure, is very important, because if you make the sashing too prominent, the central figure will not be suitably emphasized. Below is my recipe chart for the sashing to go with the wolf kachina design (see Chapter 6 on how to prepare the sashing). After cutting a piece, put a check mark next to that item so you know you have cut it.

Cut	Size	Color	What For
1	26½ x 43 in.	black	center of work
1	8 x 43 in.	teal	bottom strip
1	7 x 43 in.	tan or wolf-print	left-side strip

KEY:

W — Width
L — Length
( ) — Cutting Size
Without ( ) — Finished Size

Before Quilting:
39¼" W X 52½" L

After Quilting:
38" W X 50" L

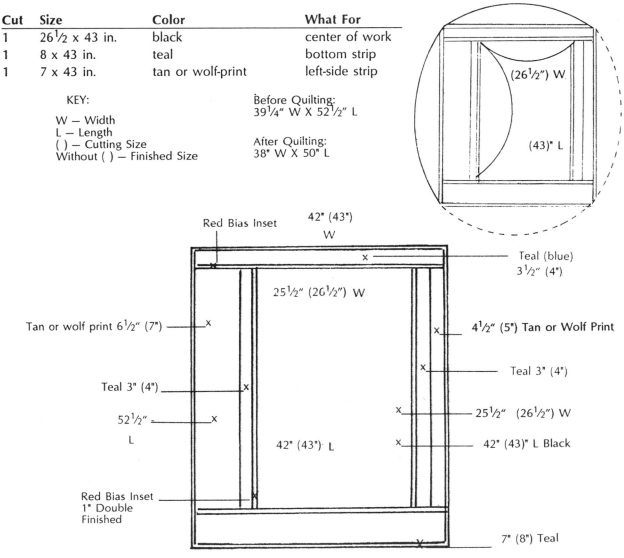

Figure 39. Wolf Background and Sashing.

Hakto, Man-Who-Carries-Wood-on-His-Head (Zuni)

This kachina appears at the First Mesa in the Bean Dance. Antelope horns and deer antlers, held in either hand, are clapped together in an appeal for a fruitful and plentiful season. Work not, want not. Colors: yellow, brown, salmon-red, white, teal, and black. The ruff is made from black and white polka-dot ribbon. Feathers, fabric tassels, shell beads, and bells were used. "Dancing kachina" fabric was a true find; I cut out the figures, backed them, and hung many about the quilt using leather strips and beads. I used the same material for the side sashing. I like to say this is my "dancing kachina" work.

Mongwa, The Great Horned Owl (Hopi)

This kachina dances in many festivals. Instead of covering his face in gray rabbit fur, I elected to use fabric wings (cut from Eagle fabric) to resemble the true feathers of an owl. Colors: yellow, red (fox ruff at neck). The striped print for the sash was taken from lengthwise striped border fabrics. The yucca whips in Mongwa's hands, often used to slap the calves of unruly children, are green. The moccasins are red with tan bottoms. Placing yucca and cactus at the right side added dimension to this quilted wall tapestry, which I corded in silver lamé and bound in black. The eyes are black pompoms on yellow circles.

Arapaho Lodgemaker (Late Nineteenth Century)

Purifying tipis and lodges with burning sage to drive away evil spirits is the practice of the lodgemaker. This ceremonial activity is still commonly practiced in today's Native American culture. The Arapaho lodgemaker is wearing distinctive body paint and a hide and cloth kilt. He wears sage on his head and carries it in both hands. I used natural colors in this work: green, lime, gray, tan, rich brown, white, yellow, and black. Feathers and beads on leather strips were put in the hair; emblems on the arms and neck were cut from another Indian print. The quilt has a double bias insert of yellow and lime. The steer skull was embroidered. When exhibiting, I attached real sage in the corresponding positions. 36 in. wide x 62 in. long

Chief Dancer (Sioux)

A Sioux chief performs a ritualistic solo dance to show his authority as tribal leader. He does this slowly and stately. I made his war bonnet with printed fabrics, which were stuffed here and there to add dimension. The fringe is of ultra-suede. Fabric colors: black, white, print, red, and orange. I sewed many Indian emblems, beads, and feathers on the headdress. 36 in. wide x 46 in long. From the collection of Mary Porter Browne, Niles, Michigan.

Clermont (Osage Chief)

Along the banks of the Arkansas River, which is now part of Oklahoma, lived the Osage Tribe. Clermont was an important chief during the 1830s, known for his wisdom and strong leadership. George Catlin, who traveled with Lewis and Clark on their famous expedition, thought a great deal of Clermont's dignity and bearing, and he left us this portrait. The possibilities obtainable from this line drawing are fantastic. Reverse appliqué would work great, embroidery on the moccasins, and so forth. This pattern would also do well on a wholecloth quilt.

Dancing Kwahu, The Eagle Kachina I (Hopi)

This dancer copies the graceful flight of the eagle, the unchallenged master of the skies. He captures the movements and rhythm of the eagle in flight. Colors: green, black, orange, yellow-red. Eagle print fabric was used on the sides, and I cut various Kwahu's from the print and appliquéd them on the work. One was filled with batting and used at the top of the quilted wall tapestry. Beads, bells, and feathers were used as embellishments. 46 in. wide x 51 in. long.

The Eagle Kachina II (Hopi)

I used this pattern from a Dover book to make my first kachina doll quilted wall tapestry. Not knowing how to proceed, I found old window shades to use for the size of pattern I needed. Piece by piece, starting with the wings, which I got carried away doing, the thing became huge. The size of the doll was 60 inches tall with a wing spread of 72 inches. My quilt size was 83 inches by 100 inches! I used three-dimensional fabric feathers at the wing bottoms, beading for the eyes, necklace, etc. The entire project, after making the pattern, took seven days to create the top and seven long days to quilt. I had at least forty needles going on this work with my "pick-up-and-go" method. If you are a beginning quilter, attempt something a bit beyond what you think you are capable of. You'll be surprised at how successful you'll be!

Right Outside Rear Feather (With Back)
Center Rear Feather (With Back)
Left Outside Rear Feather (With Back)
Top Feathers (With Back)
Head Top
Beak Top
Hand (Palm and Back)
Ear (With Back)
Head
Beak Bottom
Neck Top
Neck
Wing (With Back)
Head Bottom
Neck Bottom
Torso Top
Upper Arm
Lower Arm
Torso
Sash
Back Panel
Lower Feathers
Skirt
Side Sash Pieces
Skirt Bottom
Apron
Right Leg
Left Leg
Foot
Base Top
Base
Base Bottom

Assembled
(Front View)

Crow Mother (Hopi)

I worked the Crow Mother in the same manner as the Eagle kachina above. I put a three-dimensional straw basket in its hands with stuffed fabric printed corn. This work hangs in a gorgeous home in Ohio.

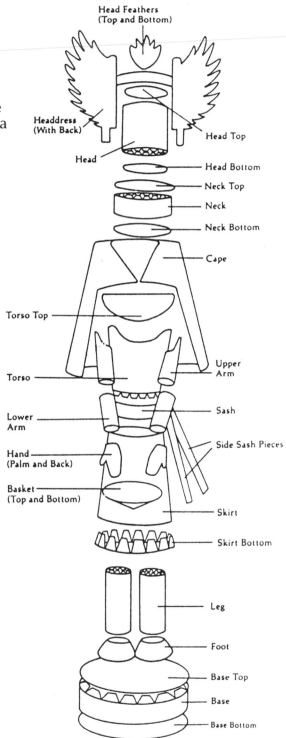

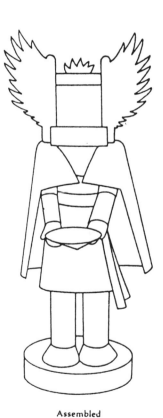

Assembled

Hano Kachina, The Clown I (Hopi, Zuni, Navajo)

As the clown, Hano brings joy to tribal ceremonies. Some are thin, but this one is a glutton. The neck sack is for corn pollen, and the hip container is his medicine pack. His favorite food is watermelon. Colors: black, white, red, green, yellow. The top and side of the hat have yellow corn tassels. For watermelons on the ground, I found a watermelon print and cut out the watermelons, which I stay-stitched and appliquéd down. I also added sequins and beads. 45 in. wide x 51 in. long

Hano Kachina, The Clown II

Hano is a clown-dancer in between serious ceremonies of the Rio Grande Pueblo tribes of New Mexico. He makes his viewers laugh with his unusual movements, which relieves the seriousness of the ceremonies. Colors: black, white, red, green. 45 in. wide x 51 in. long

Humis (or Hemis) Kachina (Hopi)

Humis is the principal figure in the Niman kachina dance, or "home dance," which is the last dance of the year. Then all the kachinas go home. His head tablet tells of clouds, rain, green grass, rainbows, and the mesa. Pine boughs are worn on his skirt and under the arm bands. The sun and moon symbols on the cheek are red. Colors: red, green, white, black, brown, and print from the sashing design. The pine boughs on the skirt and in one hand are made of silk and are three-dimensional. The rattle is a gourd. I corded this quilted wall tapestry in white and added red binding on two sides and print fabric on two sides. 47 in. wide x 80 in. long

Indian Motherhood (Navajo)

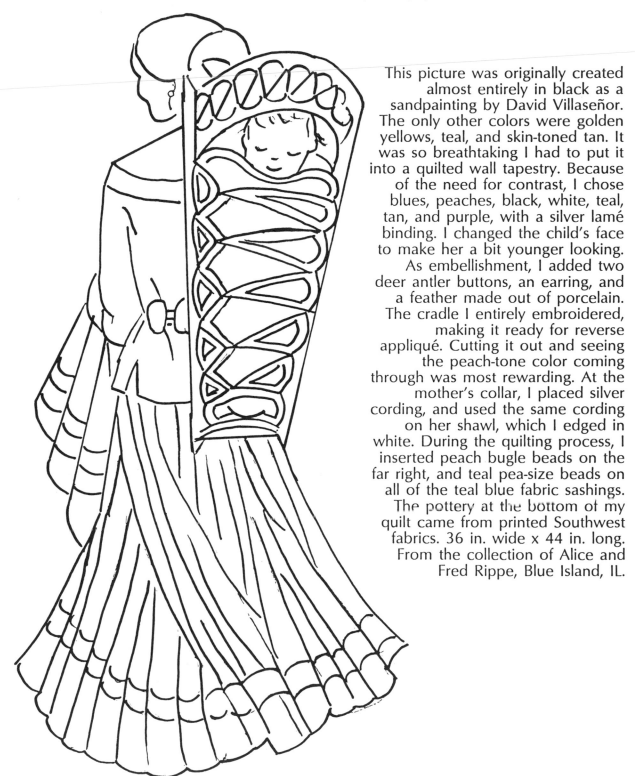

This picture was originally created almost entirely in black as a sandpainting by David Villaseñor. The only other colors were golden yellows, teal, and skin-toned tan. It was so breathtaking I had to put it into a quilted wall tapestry. Because of the need for contrast, I chose blues, peaches, black, white, teal, tan, and purple, with a silver lamé binding. I changed the child's face to make her a bit younger looking. As embellishment, I added two deer antler buttons, an earring, and a feather made out of porcelain. The cradle I entirely embroidered, making it ready for reverse appliqué. Cutting it out and seeing the peach-tone color coming through was most rewarding. At the mother's collar, I placed silver cording, and used the same cording on her shawl, which I edged in white. During the quilting process, I inserted peach bugle beads on the far right, and teal pea-size beads on all of the teal blue fabric sashings. The pottery at the bottom of my quilt came from printed Southwest fabrics. 36 in. wide x 44 in. long. From the collection of Alice and Fred Rippe, Blue Island, IL.

Father Sky and Mother Earth I (Navajo)

Father Sky on the left carries lightning strikes in his hand; he has stars and moon on his kilt; his head is curved like a rainbow. Mother Earth has corn on the left side of her kilt. Renditions vary from artist to artist. Earth tones would work well: black, white, tan, green, gold, and red-brown. A female Yei is supposed to have an oblong head, but it all depends on the artist's interpretation.

Father Sky and Mother Earth II

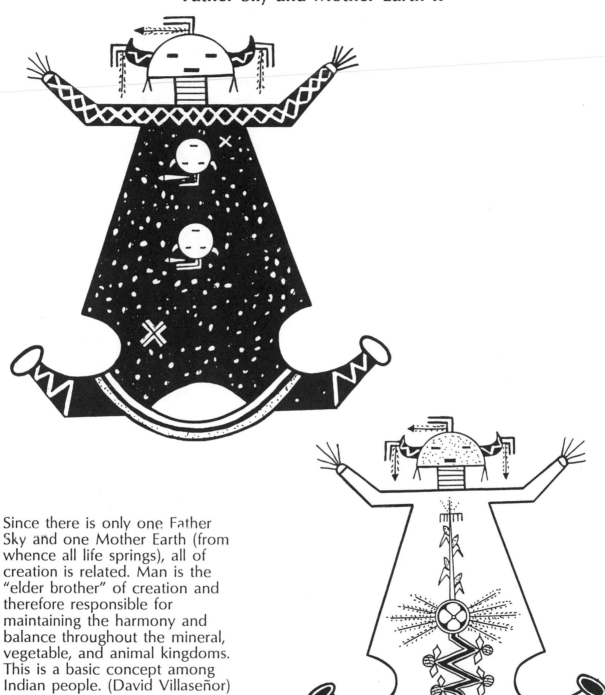

Since there is only one Father Sky and one Mother Earth (from whence all life springs), all of creation is related. Man is the "elder brother" of creation and therefore responsible for maintaining the harmony and balance throughout the mineral, vegetable, and animal kingdoms. This is a basic concept among Indian people. (David Villaseñor)

Kerwan, The Bean Planter (Hopi)

This kachina is also known as Ahaoloni or Ahulani. He dances to celebrate the return of planting-time, purification, and renovation of the earth for future planting. Bean sprouts are passed around to viewers during the dance. Colors: green, black, red, orange, white, and arrow print. White tassels are tipped with red feathers. I used a blue bias insert, white cording, and red binding. Finding a print with green beans inspired me. I cut out and stuffed the stringbeans and peas held in his hand and falling to the ground.

Macibol, The Serpent Dancer (Hopi)

These kachinas dance with live serpents about their bodies in the March festivals. I did not follow authentic Indian colors in this work, as I located a gorgeous print and borrowed the colors from it. The official colors are green mask and black zig-zag near white-rimmed eyes. Parrot and eagle feathers are on the crown. The snout, collar, bottom of kilt, and toes of moccasins are green. The blanket on the shoulder is brown, the kilt is white, and the body red. The moccasins have orange tops. The serpent is black with a white belly, with bird tracks embroidered on it. 36 in. wide x 41 in. long. From the collection of Ron and Mary B. Good, Minocqua, WI.

Momo, The Bee Kachina (Zuni)

A dancer in the Water Serpent ceremony, he imitates the hum and motions of bees. When the audience becomes unruly, he shoots blunt arrows at guilty parties. If the guilty party is a child, he appeases it with a cup of honey, which is carried on his head. Colors: black, yellow, teal, hot pink or red, white. Black and white checks represent corn. I placed silk sunflowers in the lower right corner of the quilt, which I corded in black, and bells on the leggings to chase away evil spirits. 40 in. wide x 59 in. long

Polik Mana, Butterfly Maiden (Hopi)

This beautiful kachina accompanies the towering Shalako. The ceremonial tablet worn on his head represents clouds, rain, lightning, and corn. The stripes on his face include a lot of reverse appliqué. Colors: red, green, black, brown, white, yellow, and black and white checks. My embellishments included bells, feathers, cactus, and green lamé with silk flowers. Cording the checked fabric on bias gave a special effect. Top of fabric eagle feathers are three-dimensional. 45 in. wide x 50 in. long

Eight-foot Tipi with symbols all around and eagle door. This was my first Indian quilt which led to making dozens more.

SIP-IKNE - Zuni Warrior God, Talmopya Akya, *uses yucca whips to keep crowds away from dancing Kachinas.*

Pawnee, circa 1720. *He is a warrior in battle dress, carrying real arrows for his quilted bow.*

POLIK MANA, Butterfly Maiden - Hopi *moves his body rapidly and dances in the night ceremonies.*

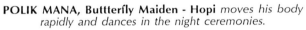

Hoop Dancer - Seminole *with hoops circling his body (sometimes flaming hoops), presents spectacular movements at festivals*

Pawnee Warrior (circa 1720)

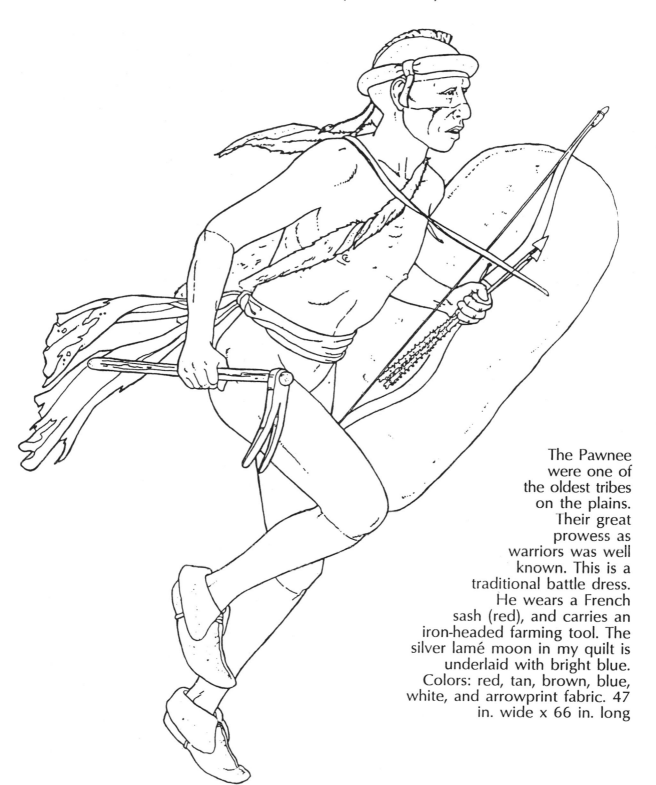

The Pawnee were one of the oldest tribes on the plains. Their great prowess as warriors was well known. This is a traditional battle dress. He wears a French sash (red), and carries an iron-headed farming tool. The silver lamé moon in my quilt is underlaid with bright blue. Colors: red, tan, brown, blue, white, and arrowprint fabric. 47 in. wide x 66 in. long

Sacagawea (Shoshone)

Sacagawea met Lewis and Clark in North Dakota. It was Hidatsa territory in 1804. She led the two American explorers westward to Shoshone country so she could go home, as she had been taken prisoner by the Hidatsa tribe. Selecting colors for this work is up to you. Yellow for the sun, moon, and stars? Brown for the fur lining? White deerskin for the cape? The cradleboard on her back could be brown. Use your imagination!

Shalako (or Salako), The Rain God (Zuni)

The Shalako ritual takes place during a forty-nine day ceremony to call rain, a house blessing, health, and the growth of plants and animals. These kachinas are about eight feet tall. The big tops are carried by dancers under many layers of capes. Accompanying the Shalako is his manager wrapped in a blanket and skull cap. He helps manipulate the wooden beak and eyes. The heavy superstructure can only be worn for a little while. Another man is always ready to replace the man inside. Capes are made with white, blue, and black; ruffs are feathers or tree sprigs. Colors: yellow, red, orange. Artificial eagle feathers are tipped in black; other bright feathers and tassels are also used. 36 in. wide x 61 in. long

Sip-Ikne (or Talmopya Akya), The Hummingbird (Zuni)

Sip-Ikne is a Zuni warrior god. A very active dancer and a guard for some kachinas, he uses his yucca branches to enforce his authority. He usually appears in the Bean Dance at the First Mesa. Colors really vary with this kachina. I chose black, red, tan, teal, and green ruffs about the ankles. The bells with fabric tassels were never worn, as the hummingbird is silent, but now he wears them. Feathers on the bird headpiece and a seashell necklace add extra charm. I made the neck ruff from a beige, black, and white print. Use a bead for the bird's eye. 56 in. wide x 76 in. long

Navajo Yei

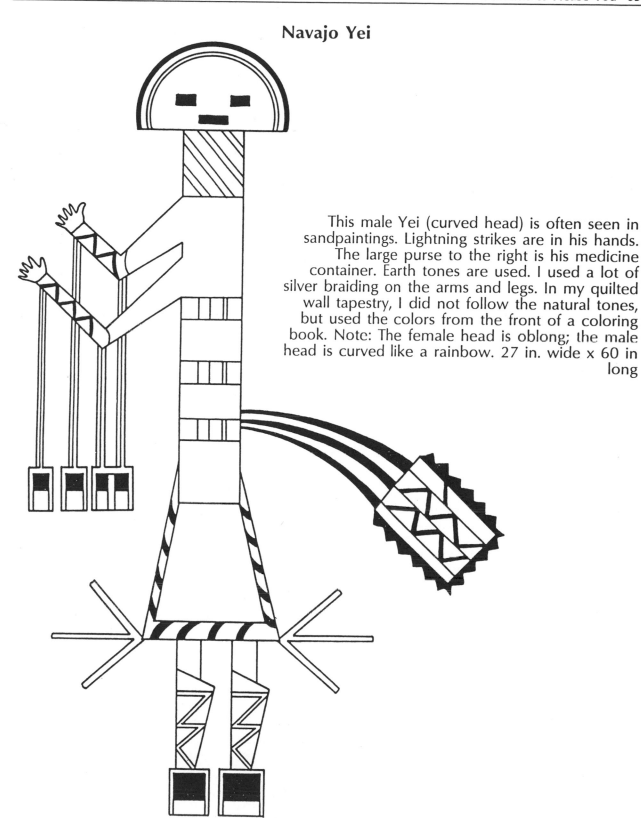

This male Yei (curved head) is often seen in sandpaintings. Lightning strikes are in his hands. The large purse to the right is his medicine container. Earth tones are used. I used a lot of silver braiding on the arms and legs. In my quilted wall tapestry, I did not follow the natural tones, but used the colors from the front of a coloring book. Note: The female head is oblong; the male head is curved like a rainbow. 27 in. wide x 60 in long

Navajo Rainbow

The opening of this rainbow always faces east. All other sides—west, north, and south—are protected so that evil may not enter.

Zuni Corn Maidens Dancing (After M. Stevenson, circa 1904)

Colors: white, black, green, red, brown, tan, etc.

A Zuni Little Dancer (After R. Bunzel, 1932)

Colors: Black, White, Green tan, Red, Teal, Yellow, Etc.

Appendix: The Quilt Frame

Just by luck, I purchased an ancient quilting frame for $6.00 years before becoming involved in this art. It was so splintered and rotten that I had it copied. Now I am able to share with you the plans for that quilt frame, which works wonderfully. Better yet, making this compact, practical, and mobile frame is simple and uncomplicated.

If you're thinking of staining and varnishing this frame, I recommend not staining the rollers if you live in a humid climate because the stain might bleed on your quilt. If you don't have the proper woodworking tools to make the traditional legs, you can use modern sawhorse caps and 2 x 4 legs. Both legs work well and can be disassembled for storage.

MATERIALS LIST FOR TWO MODELS OF FLOOR STANDING QUILT FRAMES

18	#8 or #10 1-1⅛ inch round head screws
2	2 x 4 x 38 inch pine, spruce, or harder wood boards (1½ x 3½ inches planed)
6	¾ x ¾ x 30¼ (or 1 x 1 x 30¼) inch pieces of dowel wood
2	½ x ¾ x 3 inch pieces of wood
2	1⅝ inches round x 5 feet long closet poles (or 8½–9 feet long if you want to make a larger quilt)
2	⅝ inch O.D. metal washers (optional)
2	6 x 18 inch straps from an old sheet (to be pinned to each side on the arms to give horizontal tautness)
2	strips from an old sheet: one 6 inches wide and one 20 inches wide.
4	2 inch large safety pins
4	rubber feet to fit dowels

For sawhorse legs, replace the 6 pieces of dowel wood above with the following:

4 lightweight, metal hinged sawhorse brackets (comes in sets of two) 82 x 4 x 28 inch boards (lighter duty 1 x 4 works well, too)

ASSEMBLY INSTRUCTIONS

1. Refer to Figure 40 and cut two 2 x 4 x 38 inch boards for support rails. From each end on the broad side, measure in 4 inches and at the center drill 1⅝ to 1¾ inch holes for the quilt poles. If you are making sawhorse legs, go to the next step. For traditional legs, on the bottom of each board measure in 8 inches from each end and drill ¾ x 2¼ inch deep holes angled so the legs will extend slightly away from the frame. Then in the bottom center of each board drill the same size hole angled in the opposite direction so that the middle leg will extend slightly inward (see Figure 40).

2. *Traditional legs:* Cut the dowel wood for the legs to 30¼ inches long. Round one end of each leg about 2¼ inches down so that they will fit the angled holes in the support railing without binding. If you found ¾ x ¾ inch dowel wood, the rounding may not be necessary.

Sawhorse legs: Cut 8 two-by-fours (or lighter one-by-fours if you prefer) 28 inches long for mounting into the sawhorse brackets. If you decide to use the lighter one-by-fours, then you also need to cut eight 1 x 4 x 3 inch pieces. One short and one long piece will go into each half of the bracket.

3. Take the precut closet poles and measure in 6 inches from each end. Mark and pre-drill 4 holes 90 degrees apart for 4 screws at each end of the two poles (see Figure 42).

Quilt frame stop block

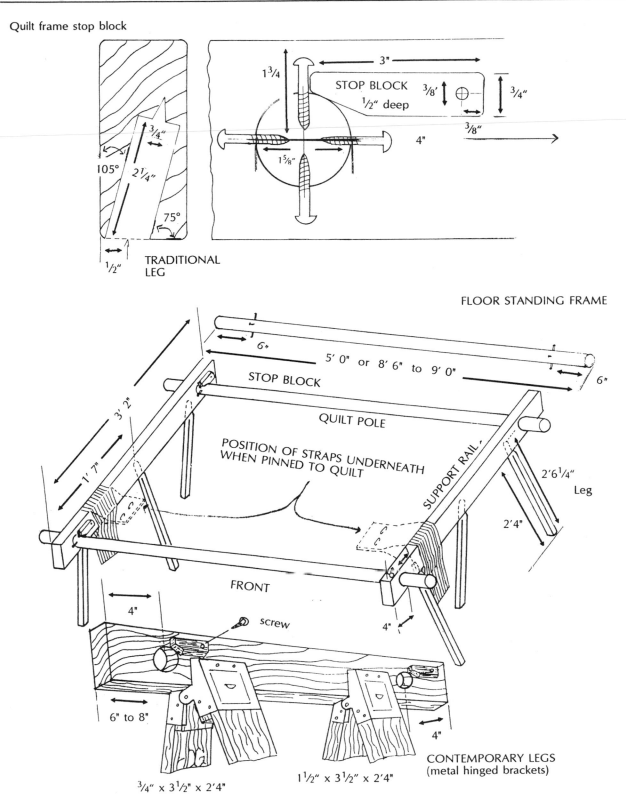

TRADITIONAL LEG

3/4"

105° 2 1/4"

75°

1/2"

STOP BLOCK
1/2" deep

1 3/4

3"

3/8'

3/4"

3/8"

1 5/8"

4"

FLOOR STANDING FRAME

STOP BLOCK

QUILT POLE

POSITION OF STRAPS UNDERNEATH
WHEN PINNED TO QUILT

SUPPORT RAIL

5' 0" or 8' 6" to 9' 0"

6"

6"

3' 2"

1' 7"

2'6 1/4"

Leg

2'4"

FRONT

4"

screw

4"

6" to 8"

3/4" x 3 1/2" x 2'4"

1 1/2" x 3 1/2" x 2'4"

4"

CONTEMPORARY LEGS
(metal hinged brackets)

Figure 40. Floor standing frame dimensions.

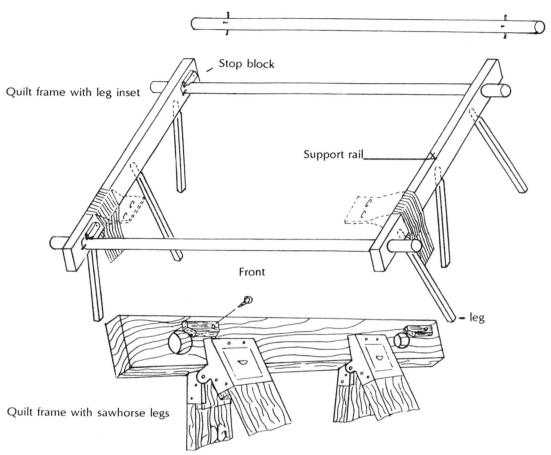

Stop block

Quilt frame with leg inset

Support rail

Front

leg

Quilt frame with sawhorse legs

Figure 41. Quilt frame with legs inset or with sawhorse legs.

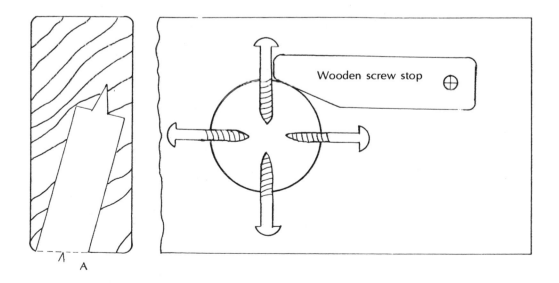

Wooden screw stop

A

Figure 42. Quilt frame stop block.

Predrill all 16 holes about ½ inch deep with a bit smaller than the diameter of the screws to be used.

4. Wrap and staple the 6-inch wide sheet to one pole, side to side, leaving a 3–4 inch tail to which your quilt will be pinned. This pole is closest to the quilter. Do the same with the second pole, except use the 20-inch wide sheet, to which the back only of the quilt will be pinned. The batting and top will be free, controlled by the side straps.

5. Refer to Figure 42 and make a tracing or measurement for the four stop blocks. Cut these and make a drill hole as shown for each piece so that the block does not bind on the screw when moved.

6. Smooth all the wood surfaces, corners, and edges with sandpaper. Stain and finish the wood (Minwax gives a soft lustre and hard finish). After the finish is dry, proceed to the next step.

7. Install the 16 screws into the quilt poles so there is ½ inch to ⅝ inch of shank between the round head and wood pole on each. This completes the quilt poles, so set them aside. Now take the support rails and lay them down so that the large quilt holes are facing up and the angled leg hole in the center is also closest to the top. Place a stop block just above and to the right of each quilt pole hole as illustrated. While holding each stop block in place, predrill a hole about ½ inch deep into the support railing with a bit smaller than the screw to be used. Place a washer over the hole, put a screw through the hole in the stop block, position it on the predrilled hole on the support railing, and tighten to the degree that the block can still pivot freely on the screw. Now you are ready for the last step.

8. Insert the traditional legs to the support rails or attach the sawhorse legs to the saw-horse brackets, and attach these to the rails. Then stand the frame upright. The stop blocks will be hanging down on the inside front and back of the side braces. Once all four ends are in, bring the rails close to the screws.

With the quilt attached to the sheeting, front and back, turn the front pole toward you until your working area is near the front where you want it. (Note: Only the bottom of the quilt sandwich is attached to the sheet at the back of the frame, then the balance must be rolled on in the opposite direction with the bulk of the roll on top of the quilt as pictured in Figure 23, page 45.) Set your front stop blocks on top against the pole screws (leaving the amount of slack in the quilt needed), and then set the rear stop blocks on top against the pole screws. Lastly, put the straps around the rails just behind the front legs and attach them to the quilt with safety pins (or straight pins may be used). They will need to be undone and reattached when you roll your work forward again on the front pole.

You are now ready to begin making your shadows of love!

But here the needle plies
Its busy task—
The pattern grows...

William Cowper, 1784

Glossary of Quilting Terms and Items

Artist's Eraser (plastic type). Used to remove pencil marks from fabric.

Backstitch. After the initial stitch, the needle is planted for the second stitch immediately behind the first stitch before stitching forward again.

Barbed Needles. Old needles with a barb on the end basically caused from polyester batting. Throw them away.

Batting (or stuffing). This is fiber placed between the top and bottom layers of a quilt.

Beard/Bearding. Batting which comes through the fabric because the weave is too loose to contain it.

Bias (of fabric). When a piece of fabric is folded at an angle to the grain, the line of the fold is known as bias.

Blended Fabrics. Amounts of cotton and polyester fibers: 50/50, 65/35, or 80/20. If the fabric contains PIMA cotton as does Palencia, which the author uses exclusively, it contains a sheen from the "combed cotton staple."

Brass Safety Pins. Use these to avoid getting rust on your work, which is a possibility with regular safety pins.

Counterpane. See wholecloth.

Fast Colors. Colors that hold permanently without fading.

Fatt Batt. This is an extra loft batting, which the author uses exclusively in her quilt work.

Fill Lines. Rule of thumb: No more than two square inches should remain unquilted on a work. Use fill quilting lines to compliment the central figure(s) and background.

Fringe. Material of ultra-suede quality which can be cut to embellish Indian quilted wall tapestries.

Lamé. A tissue-thin fabric that must have backing (underlining) when used to avoid bearding.

Loft. The thickness of batting used in quilts.

Nap (or pile). The short, fine furry texture on velveteen, velvet, corduroy, and some woolen fabrics.

Pile. See nap.

Pucker. When stay-stitching a single layer of fabric a "drawing up" or "curling" often occurs because the top machine thread, or bobbin thread, is too taut.

Pressing. Steam ironing or dry ironing a fabric. Never use steam on lamé.

Recipe Chart. Shows the fabric, colors needed, and various quilt pieces to be cut; also sashing colors and sizes; and the width and length of the main center piece. Check off from this list as each piece is cut.

Ruff. An animal skin, feather, or fabric collar used to cover necessary shoulder braces that hold large kachina head pieces in place during ceremonies.

Sandwich. The three elements that make up a quilt: (1) The top, where appliqué work has been done. (2) The batting, which is larger than the top. (3) The backing, which is the bottom of a quilt. The backing is larger than the top piece and the batting, except if using velveteen in a wholecloth situation when the sandwich is reversed.

Sashing (or stripping). Various colored strips of fabric used to frame or emphasize the central appliqué work. Similar to matting on a picture.

Selvage. A tightly woven strip on both sides of a bolt of fabric. This should be removed and never used in a quilt or bias.

Straight of Fabric. A length of fabric as it comes off a bolt of fabric.

Stay-Stitching. Using medium machine stitches on appliqué pieces to make your work easier to handle. Hand embroidery may be done instead of machine stitching.

Stripping. See sashing.

Stuffing. See batting.

Trapunto. A part of the appliqué design done in high relief by tucking in a small amount of batting from the underside, or from the topside. Leave a little space open on the appliqué into which a tiny bit of batting is placed. The work is then sewn down. This is used to hide muddy colors appearing in the background and to avoid trimming lapped appliqué where various pieces of the same material criss-cross.

Underlay. Top appliqué is lined with another fabric to give it more body, to give rosy cheeks to a complexion, or to avoid bearding.

Whip Stitching. Tacking down by hand using a backstitch. This occurs when sewing down bias binding around the edges of a work or when securing the sleeves.

Wholecloth (or counterpane). One solid piece of fabric with the quilting design only—no appliqué, piecing, or embellishments.

Width of Fabric. The area from selvage to selvage; across the fabric as it comes off the bolt.

Selected Bibliography

Bahti, Tom. *Southwest Indian Ceremonials*. K. C. Publications, 1992.

Fox, Frank, and Rita Warner. *North American Indians Coloring Album*. New York: Putnam & Grosset Group, 1978.

Gill, Sam D., and Irene F. Sullivan. *Dictionary of Native American Mythology*. New York: Oxford University Press, 1992.

Hamerstrom, Frances. *Eagles, Hawks, Falcons, and Owls of America: A Coloring Album*. Boulder: Robert Rinehart, Inc., 1984.

Heckwelder, John. *History, Manners, and Customs of the Indian Nations*. New York: Crown Publishers, 1971.

Hirschfelder, Arlene, and Pauline Nolin. *Native American Religions*. New York: M. J. K. Books, 1992.

Hunt, W. Ben. *The Complete How-To Book of Indiancraft*. New York: Macmillan Publishing Co., 1973.

LeGay, Gilbert. *Atlas of Indians of North America*. Hauppauge, New York: Barron's Educational Series, 1995.

Lyford, Carrie. *Quill and Beadwork of the Western Sioux*. Boulder: Johnson Books, 1990.

Meiczinger, John. *How to Draw Indian Arts and Crafts*. Mahwak, New Jersey: Watermill Press, 1989.

Millett, Clair Artimus. *Dancing Kachinas, Emby Originals*. Phoenix, Arizona, 1973.

Painted Tipis. (Contemporary Plains Indian Artists). Oklahoma Indian Arts and Crafts Co-op, Anadarko, Ohio, 1973.

Spence, Lewis. *Myths of the North American Indians*. New York: Random House, 1994.

Teiwes, Helga. *Kachina Dolls*. Tucson: University of Arizona Press, 1991.

Tuckman, Gail. *Through the Eyes of the Feather*. Salt Lake City: Gibbs-Smith Publisher, 1994.

Warner, Rita. *Dancing Kachinas*. Mesa, Arizona: McCreations, 1976.

Yenne, Bill, and Susan Garrett. *North American Indians*. Greenwich, Connecticut: Brampton Banks Corp., 1984.

*　　*　　*

BARNES & NOBLE, NEW YORK

Burland, Cottie. *North American Indian Mythology*. 1996.

Meadows, Kenneth. *Earth Medicine*. 1996.

Taylor, Collin. *Myths of the North American Indians*. 1995.

BELLEROPHON BOOKS, SANTA BARBARA, CALIFORNIA

A Coloring Book of American Indians. 1994.

Dutton, Berthat, and Caroline Olin. *Myths and Legends of the Indians of the Southwest: Hopi, Acomo, Tewa, Zuni*. 1994.

Great Indian Chiefs. 1994.

Myths and Legends of the Haida Indians of the Northwest. 1987.

Totem Poles. 1987.

Totem Poles to Cut and Color. Vol. 2, 1993.

DOVER PUBLICATIONS, NEW YORK

Appleton, LeRoy H. *American Indian Design and Decoration*. 1971.

Catlin, George. *North American Indians*. Vols. 1 and 2. 1971.

Copeland, Peter F. *Woodland Indians Coloring Book*. 1995.

Fewkes, Avenel, and Jesse Walter. *Hopi Kachinas*. 1985.

Green, John. *Indian Life in Pre-Columbian North America Coloring Book*. 1994.

Kennedy, Paul E. *North American Indian Design Coloring Book*. 1971.

Orban-Szontagh, Madeleine. *North American Indian Designs, Iron-On Transfer Patterns*. 1991.

Reichard, Gladys A. *Navajo Medicine Man Paintings*. 1977.

Richman, David. *Plains Indian Coloring Book*. 1983.

Smith, A. G., and Josie Hazen. *Cut and Make Kachina Dolls*. 1992.

Smith-Sides, Dorothy. *Decorative Art of the Southwestern Indians*. 1961.

FUN PUBLISHING COMPANY, SCOTTSDALE, ARIZONA

Greenlee, Donna. *The Kachina Doll Book*, No. 2. 1973.

___ *The Plains Indian Book*. 1974.

GRAMERCY BOOKS, AVENEL, NEW YORK

Curtis, Natalie. *The Indian Book*. 1987.

Linderman, Frank B. *Blackfeet Indians*. 1995.

NATUREGRAPH PUBLISHERS, HAPPY CAMP, CALIFORNIA

Cuevas, Lou. *Apache Legends: Songs of the Wind Dancer*. 1991.

Villaseñor, David. *Tapestries in Sand: The Spirit of Indian Sandpaintings*. 1966.

Villaseñor, David and Jean. *Indian Designs*. 1983.

NORTHLAND PUBLISHING, FLAGSTAFF, ARIZONA

Wright, Barton. *Clowns of the Hopi*. 1994.

_____ *Hopi Kachinas*. 1992.

_____ *Kachinas*. 1991.

TREASURE CHEST PUBLICATIONS, TUCSON, ARIZONA

Asch, Connie. *Kachina Coloring Book*. 1982.

Branson, Oscar T. *Hopi Indian Kachina Dolls*. 1992.

Joe, Eugene Baatsoslanii, and Mark Bahti. *Navajo Sandpainting Art*. 1978.

UNIVERSITY OF NEW MEXICO PRESS, ALBUQUERQUE, NEW MEXICO

Colton, Harold S. *Hopi Kachina Dolls*. 1959.

Fergusson, Erna. *Dancing Gods: Indian Ceremonials of New Mexico and Arizona*. 1964.